ROBIN GAULDIE

EYEWITNESS TRAVEL

Left **Dolphin fresco, Knosos** Right **Rethymno harbour**

LONDON, NEW YORK,
MELBOURNE, MUNICH AND DELHI
www.dk.com

Produced by Blue Island Publishing
Printed and bound in China

First published in the UK in 2003
by Dorling Kindersley Limited
80 Strand, London WC2R 0RL
A Penguin Random House Company

17 18 10 9 8 7 6 5 4 3

Copyright 2003, 2015
© **Dorling Kindersley Limited, London**
Reprinted with revisions
2005, 2007, 2009, 2011, 2013, 2015

A CIP catalogue record is available from the
British Library.

ISBN 978-0-24100-749-5

Within each Top 10 list in this book, no
hierarchy of quality or popularity is implied.
All 10 are, in the editor's opinion, of roughly
equal merit.

MIX
Paper from
responsible sources
FSC
www.fsc.org   FSC™ C018179

Contents

Crete's Top 10

The information in this DK Eyewitness Top 10 Travel Guide is checked regularly.
Every effort has been made to ensure that this book is as up-to-date as possible at the time of
going to press. Some details, however, such as telephone numbers, opening hours, prices,
gallery hanging arrangements and travel information are liable to change. The publishers cannot
accept responsibility for any consequences arising from the use of this book, nor for any
material on third party websites, and cannot guarantee that any website address in this book
will be a suitable source of travel information. We value the views and suggestions of our
readers very highly. Please write to: Publisher, DK Eyewitness Travel Guides,
Dorling Kindersley, 80 Strand, London WC2R 0RL, UK, or email: travelguides@dk.com

Key to abbreviations
Adm *admission charge payable* **Free** *no admission charge*

Left **Plakias** Right **Tavernas, Chersonisos**

Around the Island

Streetsmart

Contents

Left **Castle, Paleochora** Right **Siteia harbour**

Following pages **Siteia beach**

CRETE'S
TOP 10

CRETE'S TOP 10

Highlights of Crete

Although it could not be more Greek, Crete is really a country within a country, with its own history, folklore and traditions. It was the birthplace of Europe's oldest civilization, the enigmatic Minoan culture which flourished over 4,000 years ago. Greeks, Romans, Byzantines, Saracens, Venetians and Turks also left their mark. This rich human heritage is set against the backdrop of magnificent mountain scenery and beaches lapped by a deep blue sea.

Irakleio
A good place to see a slice of everyday Greek street life, Crete's capital is an eclectic mix of medieval Venetian fortifications, bustling markets and modern streets *(see pp12–13)*.

Ancient Knosos
Knosos is among the most impressive relics of the ancient Mediterranean world. The Minoan palace was imaginatively reconstructed in the early 20th century *(see pp8–11)*.

Irakleio Archaeological Museum
Crete's leading museum houses amazing finds from Knosos and other great archaeological sites *(see pp14–15)*.

Chania
Once the island's capital, this pretty little harbour town, with good beaches nearby and lots of open-air restaurants and shops, makes a great base for exploring Crete's wild west *(see pp18–19)*.

Phaestos
One of the most important Minoan palace sites in Crete, Phaestos is a fascinating maze of walls, stairways and courtyards on a hillside overlooking the Messara plain and the Libyan Sea *(see pp20–21)*.

Rethymno
6 Crete's third largest city is packed with reminders of a multi-layered history. A huge castle, Turkish mosques, Venetian town houses and bustling markets are part of the charm, along with a beach esplanade *(see pp22–3)*.

Gortys
7 The bases of toppled Roman columns, the ruins of a Byzantine basilica, post-Minoan fortifications, an agora, acropolis and remains of temples to Athena and Apollo all hint at the chequered past of Gortys *(see pp24–5)*.

Samaria Gorge
8 The "White Mountains" of the Sfakia region dominate southwest Crete. This rugged massif, most of which can only be explored on foot, as there are few roads, is cloaked in pine trees and traversed by the lovely Samaria Gorge *(see pp26–7)*.

The Amari Valley & Mt Idi
9 Old-fashioned villages, empty mountain panoramas and legend-laden caves seem like part of a different world, and can easily be explored with a rented car or escorted coach tour *(see pp28–9)*.

Gournia
10 The best preserved Minoan town on Crete has a honeycomb-like labyrinth of tiny houses and narrow lanes surrounding a small palace overlooking the Gulf of Mirabello *(see pp30–31)*.

Ancient Knosos

Knosos is steeped in mystery and enchantment. In legend, it was the seat of King Minos, beneath whose palace the bull-headed Minotaur hunted its victims in the labyrinth built by Daedalus. In reality, it was the hub of a Bronze Age empire that held sway over the Aegean more than 4,000 years ago. This part of the Knosos story only began to be unearthed at the beginning of the 20th century, when British archaeologist Sir Arthur Evans began excavations of the site.

Dolphin Frescoes

3 The queen's rooms were lavishly decorated with frescoes of leaping dolphins and well equipped with a bath and even a flush lavatory.

Central court

🕐 If possible, visit Knosos in spring or autumn, when cooler weather makes exploring more pleasant than in high summer. But if you are holidaying in peak season, get to the site as soon as it opens, before most coach tour groups have arrived.

🍴 There are several tavernas and snack bars within a few steps of the site entrance, along the main road to Irakleio.

• Map K4 • Route 97, 5 km (8 miles) south of Irakleio • 28102 31940
• Summer: 8am–8pm daily (last entry 7pm); winter: 8am–3pm daily
• Closed some national holidays • Adm €6; concessions €3; combined ticket for Knosos and Irakleio Archaeological Museum (see pp14–15) €10
• Disabled access difficult

Top 10 Sights

1. Central Court
2. Piano Nobile
3. Dolphin Frescoes
4. Storehouses
5. South Portico
6. Great Staircase
7. Hall of Double Axes
8. North Entrance Passage
9. Throne Room
10. Bust of Sir Arthur Evans

Central Court

1 All Minoan palaces were built around a central courtyard. This would have been the hub of the complex and would probably have been used for ceremonial purposes and for royal audiences. The courtyard of Knosos has a commanding view of the valley.

Piano Nobile

2 Evans dubbed this expansive room on the upper floor of the palace building the "noble hall", believing that it might have been the audience hall of the ancient Minoan kings. Its walls are decorated with copies of the fabulous frescoes of agile, leaping bull dancers – the most famous images of Knosos.

Storehouses

4 The storehouses or "magazines" contain giant earthenware jars called *pithoi*, which the Minoans used to store olive oil, olives, grain and other supplies. Such jars, with a capacity of up to 200 litres, were used by later Greeks over the next four millennia, and are still made today.

Plan of Knosos

5 South Portico
The imposing south gateway to the palace complex has been partially restored, and is decorated with copies of the flowing Procession fresco, the original of which (like the other dazzling finds from Knosos) may be seen in the Irakleio Archaeological Museum *(see pp14–15)*. The roof of this porch was originally supported by four tapering wooden columns.

6 Great Staircase
Three smaller stairways and a maze of corridors would once have led off the five broad, shallow stone steps of the grand staircase. Four of these wide steps survive, and a copy of the original Shield fresco which was found here decorates this part of the palace complex.

7 Hall of Double Axes
The hallway leading to the King's chamber is named after the double-bladed axe symbols *(above)* carved into its walls and columns. The double axe was a characteristic symbol of Knosos and its empire.

8 North Entrance Passage
A fresco of a charging bull, one of the enduring symbols of Knosos, adorns the entrance to this passage. Either side of the entrance are ruined chambers and deep stone storage pits. Images of sacred bulls outlasted the enigmatic Minoan civilization and helped foster the legend of the Minotaur.

9 Throne Room
Here, a stone throne – supposedly that of King Minos – stands next to a basin. The basin is believed to have been used for ritual purification, perhaps before sacrifices were made to honour the gods.

10 Bust of Sir Arthur Evans
A bust of Evans stands at the site entrance, honouring the man who first traced the legendary palace of King Minos to this hillside above Irakleio. His broad reconstructions of the ancient palace owe much to his imagination.

Many of the exhibits at Knosos are copies – the originals are preserved at the Irakleio Archaeological Museum See pp14–15

Left **Central Court, Knosos** Centre **Horns of Consecration, Knosos** Right **View of Gournia**

Archaeologists in Crete

1 Arthur Evans

Arthur Evans was born into a wealthy British family and educated at Oxford, where he later became keeper of the prestigious Ashmolean Museum. Crete's liberation from Turkish rule in 1897, three years after his first visit to the site, made it possible for him to begin work in 1900, and he devoted the next three decades to Knosos.

2 Harriet Boyd-Hawes

Harriet Boyd (Boyd-Hawes following her marriage) arrived on Crete in 1901 and, after hunting for promising sites, surprised the archaeological world by unearthing at Gournia a complete Minoan town (see pp30–31).

3 Nikolaos Platon

The instincts of Greek archaeologist Nikolaos Platon led to the rediscovery in 1961–2 of the unplundered, overlooked palace site at Zakros (see p35). The important clue was the natural harbour – Platon suspected the site had once been an important trading city.

Agia Triada

4 John Pendlebury

Pendlebury, who continued Evans's work at Knosos, is one of the most colourful figures in Cretan archaeology. He explored much of the island on foot and by donkey, pinpointing dozens of important sites. He also became a hero to Cretans after dying in action against the invading Germans in 1941.

5 Federico Halbherr

An Italian, Halbherr came to Crete in 1884 and befriended the Cretan archaeologist Joseph Hadzidakis, with whom he discovered the Bronze Age relics at the Diktian Cave (see p80). He later unearthed the palace sites at Phaestos (see pp20–21) and Agia Triada (see p81).

6 Richard Seager

Among the first American scholars to work in Crete, where at the beginning of the 20th century he excavated the Minoan site at Vasiliki, before starting work at Mochlos (see p105), where American archaeologists are still at work together with Greek researchers.

7 Joseph Hadzidakis

Crete's own Joseph Hadzidakis pioneered the search for relics of the island's distant past, winning permission from the Ottoman sultan to set up the Cretan Archaeological Society in the 1880s. The Society played a key role in locating and preserving

For more on the ancient sites in Crete **See pp34–5**

Phaestos

Crete's important sites, and in setting up the Irakleio Archaeological Museum *(see pp14–15)*.

Alan Wace
The prominent director of the British School at Athens, Wace clashed with the opinionated Arthur Evans when his discoveries at Mycenae on the mainland led him to claim (correctly) that the Mycenaean culture had not been an offshoot of the Minoan but had existed independently and eventually had come to control Knosos.

Minos Kalokairinos
Cretan businessman and amateur archaeologist Kalokairinos began the first dig at Knosos in 1878, finding fragments of Mycenaean pottery and large pottery storage jars. His discoveries brought Knosos to the attention of Heinrich Schliemann.

Heinrich Schliemann
A rich and famous archaeologist fascinated with the world of Homer's epics, he discovered first the site of ancient Troy (in Turkey), then Mycenae (in mainland Greece). In 1887, he turned his attention to Crete, but died before his researches could bear fruit, leaving the field open for Arthur Evans.

The Discovery of Knosos

Bust of Sir Arthur Evans

Arthur Evans was inspired to dig at Knosos by the great German archaeologist Heinrich Schliemann, whose death in 1890 prevented him from excavating the site of what he was convinced was a major Minoan palace. Evans, who excavated the long-lost Minoan palace at Knosos between 1900 and 1929, stands accused by some archaeologists of having used rather too much imagination in his reconstruction of the site, and especially of the upper floor which he dubbed the "Piano Nobile". That said, Evans was attempting to bring to life a site whose origins were lost in the mists of time, and his guesswork is perhaps excusable. Along with the brilliant artistry of the long dead Minoan fresco-painters whose work decorates the walls, his lively imagination at least makes Knosos one of the most colourful and fascinating ruins in Greece.

Queen's Bath
The reconstruction of the clay bath is typical of the conjecture about the function of the rooms at Knosos. Minoan civilization was clearly sophisticated, but did the bath really belong to a queen, as Evans claimed?

Irakleio

A massive medieval fortress still guards the harbour where the galleys of the Serene Republic of Venice once moored. Centuries-old churches and drinking fountains are other reminders of Irakleio's Venetian era. Busy open-air markets and the island's most fascinating museum are also attractions. Find a café table on one of the central squares and watch the busy everyday life of a small Greek town, or browse the markets for Cretan antiques and delicacies to take home.

Venetian Arsenal

The great wooden war-galleys that gave Venice its maritime supremacy were built and repaired in vaulted arcades *(above)* on the harbourfront opposite the fortress. Wooden fishing boats are still hauled up here for maintenance.

Plateia Venizelou

🕐 To see the market at its best, arrive early, when the stalls are still piled high. The market remains open all day, Monday to Saturday, but most produce traders have packed up by midday.

🍷 Plateia Venizelou is lined with pavement cafés and a good place for a cold drink and a rest after a morning exploring the market and city.

Map K3 • Greek
National Tourism
Organisation, 1
Xanthoudidou
• 28102 46299
• 9am–3pm Mon–Fri

Top 10 Sights

1. Archaeological Museum
2. Venetian Fortress (Koules)
3. Venetian Arsenal
4. Historical Museum of Crete
5. Morosini Fountain
6. Market
7. Museum of Religious Art
8. Natural History Museum
9. Museum of the Battle of Crete
10. Venetian Bastions

Irakleio harbour

Historical Museum of Crete

The museum's proudest possession is the only painting by El Greco to have been retained in the artist's native Crete. There are also some lovely stone pieces *(below; see p83)*.

Archaeological Museum

Irakleio's Archaeological Museum is one of the finest in Greece, with finds from ancient Minoan, Greek and Roman cities *(above; see pp14–15)*.

Venetian Fortress (Koules)

The massive walls of the square fortress – the most imposing historic building in Irakleio – were strengthened by the Venetians as the Turkish threat grew during the 16th century.

For a morning's walk in Irakleio See pp82–3

Morosini Fountain

Carved stone lions, the symbol of St Mark, decorate a small fountain *(above)* in the hub of Irakleio's old quarter. It is named after a great 17th-century Doge of Venice. Sadly, it is often dry.

Market

The old market has striped awnings and counters piled high with everything from live snails to a myriad varieties of olive *(right)*.

Museum of Religious Art

The world's finest collection of Cretan icons is displayed in a pretty 15th-century church *(below)*. Colourful, glowing depictions of saints and martyrs, some of them in elaborate silver frames, adorn the walls. There are three works by Michailis Damaskinos: the *Adoration of the Magi*, *Last Supper*, and *Christ Appearing to the Holy Women*.

Natural History Museum

Offers an impression of the Cretan landscape in Minoan times, before the importation of palm trees, eucalyptus and bougainvillea. There are also stuffed animals, fossils and crystals.

Museum of the Battle of Crete

This small collection highlights the German invasion of 1941 and the Cretan resistance to German occupation from 1941–45. There are photographs, documents, weapons and uniforms.

Venetian Bastions

Irakleio's Venetian walls *(above)* are surprisingly intact, though among a concrete tide of modern buildings. The best place to appreciate the fortifications is from outside the Chania Gate, with its elaborate carving. Next to it is the massive Pantokratoros Bastion.

Irakleio's Story

The Saracens who occupied Crete in the 9th and 10th centuries built a stronghold on the site of an earlier Roman-Greek settlement named Irakleio after the Greek hero Herakles (Hercules). Under Venetian rule, the name was corrupted into Candia. It reverted to its original name after independence from Turkey. The city was heavily damaged by bombing during World War II, but rose again to become Crete's official capital in 1971.

Irakleio Archaeological Museum

Founded in 1937 to house the growing treasury of finds from Crete's newly rediscovered archaeological sites, Irakleio's Archaeological Museum gives a dazzling insight into the marvels of the first sophisticated European civilization, which flourished on this island more than 3,000 years ago. Among the most famous and striking exhibits are the frescoes from Knosos, jewellery, symbol seals and Minoan double axes, as well as the enigmatic Phaestos Disc, with its symbols written by people of the ancient world.

Minoan Jewellery and Helmets

Gold necklaces, pendants (above), rings, seals, sword hilts and helmets are among the many finds from Knosos, Phaestos and Gortys.

An exhibit at the Irakleio Archaeological Museum

The museum is a must-see for anyone interested in the rich history of Crete. This world-class facility contains artifacts from all over Greece, and includes several important finds from most of the major antiquity sites in Crete.

Plateia Eleftherias, near the museum, is pedestrianized and has a row of café terraces.

Plateia Eleftherias/1 Xanthoudidou 711, Irakleio • 28102 79000 • Apr–Oct: 8am–8pm daily; Nov–Mar: 11am–5pm Mon, 8am–3pm Tue–Sun & public hols. • Closed some public holidays. • Adm €6; concessions €3

Top 10 Exhibits

1. Ayia Triada Sarcophagus
2. Hall of Frescoes
3. Minoan Jewellery and Helmets
4. Faience Figurines of the Snake Goddess
5. Bull's Head Rhyton
6. Jug of Reeds
7. Miniature Figures
8. Gaming Board
9. Phaestos Disc
10. Town Mosaic

Ayia Triada Sarcophagus

This elaborately painted stone coffin is adorned with depictions of animal sacrifices, a funeral procession (main image), women riding chariots pulled by slaves, and mythical beasts. It was perhaps made for a Minoan ruler.

Hall of Frescoes

The most exciting and impressive of the museum's displays are the lively, colourful frescoes from Knosos, Agia Triada and other palaces. They seem to offer a real link between the past and present.

Faience Figurines of the Snake Goddess

Found at Knosos, these figures (left) carry a snake in either hand, as do some later depictions of the goddess Astarte, suggesting some continuity between ancient Crete and later Hellenic cultures. The figurines were discovered by Sir Arthur Evans, who considered them as possible evidence of a matriarchal society.

5 Bull's Head Rhyton

Fashioned in the shape of a bull's head, this 16th-century BC wine vessel *(right)* is carved from black steatite stone and has gilded horns, rock crystal eyes and a mother-of-pearl snout. It was discovered at Knosos and probably used in ritual.

6 Jug of Reeds

With its dark pattern of reeds painted on a lighter background, this graceful pottery jug is the finest example of work from the New Palace era (1700–1450 BC).

7 Miniature Figures

Doll-like figurines of people and animals *(below)* look like toys but are believed to have had a religious purpose as votive offerings. Most were found in mountain sanctuaries and caves, such as the Diktian (Psychro) Cave *(see p80)*. The figures give an important insight into contemporary fashions, along with an indication of gestures of worship.

9 Phaestos Disc

This clay disc *(below)* is embossed with symbols believed to be the earliest example of a form of printing. The hieroglyphics on the disc, which were found at Phaestos in 1903, are the earliest known Minoan script.

8 Gaming Board

A decorative gaming board, elaborately inlaid and decorated with rock crystal, gold and silver leaf, turquoise paste and ivory, shows that ancient Crete had a wealthy, leisured class as well as trade links with other ancient civilizations.

10 Town Mosaic

Glazed tiles, each depicting multi-storey buildings of the Minoan era, were originally part of a mural decoration that may have graced the wall of a palace.

Museum Guide

Works to modernize and extend the museum completed in 2014, to reveal the largest museum in Greece, and one of the largest museums of Minoan art in the world. The new, world-class facility houses a collection that spans 7,500 years in 24 rooms. It occupies approximately 3,000 sq m (32,300 sq ft). Exhibits, comprising artifacts, mosaics, statues and beautiful wall paintings, are displayed both chronologically, as well as according to themes. There is a museum shop and a café in the building as well.

🔟 Chania

Chania is Crete's prettiest (and second largest) town, with colourful old Venetian buildings ringing a sheltered harbour that is guarded by sturdy fortifications. To the south are the treeless peaks of the Lefka Ori (White Mountains), sometimes snow-covered to June. Good beaches lie to the west and on the Akrotiri peninsula to the east. As well as Venetian ramparts and churches, a scattering of old Turkish buildings are reminders of the 250 years of Turkish rule.

Municipal Market

Café on Kondylaki

🛍 Chania is the best shopping spot on Crete. Designer beachwear and silver jewellery are in shops on Chalidon and the harbour. Cretan-style leather boots are found in cobbler's shops on Skridlof. The Cretan House Folklore Museum sells beautiful handicrafts.

🍴 The priciest and noisiest restaurants line Akti Koundouriotou, the harbour esplanade. For cheap eats, try the streets east of Plateia Sindrivani.

Map D2 • Municipality Information Office, next to the town hall, 28213 41666, 8:30am–2:30pm Mon–Sat • Firkas 9am–5pm Mon–Sat, 10am–6pm Sun • Museums Tue–Sun • Market 7am–noon Mon–Sat

Top 10 Sights

1. Firkas
2. Chania Archaeological Museum
3. Municipal Market
4. Cretan House Folklore Museum
5. Mosque of the Janissaries
6. Byzantine Collection
7. Etz Hayyim Synagogue
8. Schiavo Bastion and Venetian Walls
9. Lighthouse
10. "Oasis Beach"/Kalamaki

Atmospheric alleyway in Chania

Firkas
Built to guard the harbour, this massive bastion now houses an eclectic Naval Museum *(above)*, including a display about the Battle of Crete.

Chania Archaeological Museum
The excellent collection includes Minoan pottery and clay tablets, Classical and Hellenistic sculpture and glassware, and some fine mosaics *(right)*.

Municipal Market
The market, housed in a 19th-century building, is best visited first thing in the morning. Local farm produce is piled high, including weird-looking fish on beds of ice. There is every imaginable variety of olive, herb and spice.

Previous pages **Rethymno harbour**

Cretan House Folklore Museum

With its collection of tools, looms, spinning wheels, rugs, wall hangings and embroidery, this museum reveals and preserves traditional Cretan village skills *(see also p39)*.

Mosque of the Janissaries

The Turks built this multi-domed building *(above)* to set their stamp on Crete after the conquest of 1645. It is the oldest Ottoman building on the island.

Byzantine Collection

Next to the Firkas, the Byzantine Collection covers the 1,000-year history of the Byzantine Empire, with displays of coins, jewellery and statuary, mosaics and some fine icons.

Etz Hayyim Synagogue

The 15th-century synagogue was used by Chania's Jewish population until the German occupation of 1941–45, when they were deported to death camps by the Germans. A plaque bears the names of 376 Jews who died when a deportees' ship was inadvertently sunk by a British submarine.

Schiavo Bastion and Venetian Walls

The massive Schiavo Bastion and the high walls either side of it are the best preserved of the landward section of the Venetian fortifications, built in the mid-15th century as the threat of Turkish invasion loomed. (No public access.)

"Oasis Beach"/ Kalamaki

The beach, between the Chrissi Akti headland and Kalamaki, about 3 km (2 miles) from the city centre, is the best near Chania, with its long curve of sand and shingle, cafés and restaurants, parascending and water sports.

Lighthouse

Walk out to the little lighthouse at the tip of the Venetian harbour wall *(above)* for a fine view of the waterfront, harbour entrance and city.

Chania's Story

Chania's earliest settlers were Minoans. Later, in 520 BC, colonists from Samos arrived. From 1252 until 1645, it was mainly ruled by the Venetians, who fortified the town and harbour. However, Chania fell in 1645 after a 55-day siege and remained in Turkish hands until 1898. In World War II, Cretan civilians fought alongside Greek and British Commonwealth troops. The German garrison in Chania held out until May 1945.

10 Phaestos

While Arthur Evans was reconstructing Knosos, the more meticulously scientific Italian scholar Federico Halbherr was unearthing the sites of two Minoan palaces at Phaestos, on a hilltop above the fertile farmlands of the Messara Plane. Most of the ruins visible today are remnants of the later palace (known as the Second Palace), built around 1600 BC and destroyed, possibly by a tidal wave, in around 1450 BC.

Central Court

3 This vast courtyard *(above)*, formerly flanked on two sides by covered walkways, may have been a parade ground. Niches, perhaps for sentries, are recessed into walls by the main entrance.

Top 10 Sights

Grand Stairway

🔵 The on-site Tourist Pavilion at Phaestos serves cold drinks and indifferent food, but there are several better (and cheaper) refreshments stops at Agios Ioannis village, including the Taverna Agios Ioannis, on the main street.

✪ For an overnight stop, head for the little resort of Matala, with sandy beaches and small hotels, less than 30 minutes drive from Phaestos.

• Map H5 • 8 km (5 miles) west of Moires village • 28920 42315 • Summer: 8am–8pm daily; winter: 8am–3pm daily. • Closed on national holidays. • Adm €4; combined ticket with Agia Triada (see p81): €6

West Courtyard and Theatre Area

1 Tiers of stone seats *(below)* occupy the north side of the West Court-yard, a paved space that was used for rituals and theatrical ceremonies, including, perhaps, the bull-vaulting depicted in some Minoan frescoes. South of the courtyard are two well-like stone-lined pits used for storing grain, and in the northeast corner are the remains of a shrine which was part of the earlier palace.

Grand Stairway

2 This broad, monumental stairway leads from the West Courtyard up to the remains of a propylon, or portico, and into a colonnaded lightwell. This was the main entrance to the palace.

Discover more at www.traveldk.com

Peristyle Hall
The stumps of columns lining this square space indicate that it was once a colonnaded courtyard. Beneath it are traces of an even more archaic building, dating from what is known as the Prepalatial period (3500–1900 BC).

Archive
This row of mud-brick coffers may have been the filing department. The Phaestos Disc, with its undeciphered hieroglyphics, was discovered here. It can be seen in the Irakleio Archaeological Museum (see pp14–15).

Plan of Phaestos

Storerooms and Pithoi
The storerooms (above) were where essentials such as grain, oil, wine and olives were kept in huge ceramic jars called pithoi. Several pithoi remain in the storerooms.

First Palace Remains
To the southeast of the site, the smaller ruins of the First Palace are fenced off for their protection. The palace was built c.1900 BC and destroyed about 200 years later.

Palace Workshops
The remains of a sophisticated kiln or bronze-smith's furnace stand in a large courtyard. Off the courtyard are small chambers which may have been workshops for the palace artisans.

Classical Temple
The remnants of a small temple built during the Classical era provide evidence that Phaestos was still lived in some 1000 years after the mysterious collapse of the Minoan civilization.

Royal Apartments
Now fenced off, these rooms were the grandest in the complex, consisting of the Queen's Chamber, the King's Chamber, a lustral basin (covered pool), and even a bathroom and lavatory with running water (above).

Minoan Demise
What caused the sudden collapse of the Minoan civilisation? Many believe that it was the eruption of the volcano on the island of Thira (Santorini), which would have triggered great tidal waves and suffocating clouds of volcanic ash. Other explanations include invasion by the warlike Mycenaeans of the mainland. But all such theories remain speculative for now.

Rethymno

Rethymno, Crete's third largest town, has been occupied since Minoan times and flourished under Venetian rule. Built on a wide, shallow bay, it has a good beach at the heart of town, and an old quarter crammed with the tall windows and wrought-iron balconies of old-fashioned Venetian and Turkish houses. Several well-preserved mosques are relics of the Turkish era, and, along with the palm trees planted along its seafront esplanade, give the town a pleasantly exotic atmosphere.

Historical and Folk Art Museum

Vivid woven rugs and hangings *(above)*, fine lace, traditional pottery and magnificent silver and amber jewellery are among the relics of a vanished way of life preserved in this small museum. Richly decorated textiles from the Franzeskaki collection are also displayed.

Venetian Gate

🕐 Visit Rethymno in July to enjoy the annual wine festival in the public gardens.

🍴 Rethymno's bustling harbour front caters almost exclusively for tourists. Head for the quiet alleys of the old quarter for cheaper, less crowded and often more authentically Cretan restaurants.

Map F3 • Rethymno Tourist Information Office, Sofokli Venizelou 28310 29148 • 8am–2:30pm Mon–Fri • Fortress 8:30am–8:30pm in summer; for winter hours, call 28310 28101 • Adm €4; family ticket €10; over 65s €3; children, students and disabled visitors free • Museums Tue–Sun

Top 10 Sights

1. Venetian Fortress
2. Historical and Folk Art Museum
3. Nerandzes Mosque
4. Rethymno Archaeological Museum
5. Rimondi Fountain
6. Venetian Loggia
7. Municipal Gardens
8. Inner Harbour
9. Venetian Gate
10. Beach

Venetian Fortress (Fortetza)

Built in 1573, this imposing stronghold – one of the largest Venetian castles ever built – broods on a headland above the town. It has four sturdy bastions and three gates. Within the walls, the most interesting building is the Ibrahim Han Mosque *(below)*, originally the Venetian Cathedral *(see p40)*.

Rethymno's inner harbour

Nerandzes Mosque (Odeion)

Rising above the old town's rooftops, the pointed minaret of the 17th-century Nerandzes Mosque is a prominent landmark of Rethymno. It is now a music college. Once a Latin church, it was converted into a mosque by the Turks, who replaced the roof with cupolas and the bell tower with a minaret.

For a morning's itinerary in Rethymno See pp94–5

4 Rethymno Archaeological Museum

Opposite the main gate of the fortress, in a converted bastion (part of the fortifications added by the Turks), the archaeological museum's displays include finds from Neolithic, Minoan and Roman sites *(left; see p36)*.

5 Rimondi Fountain

Water flows from an ornate fountain, built in 1626 by one of Rethymno's patrician families on the site of an earlier, simpler water source. Both Venetians and Turks endowed various cities with numerous public fountains.

6 Venetian Loggia (Lotzia)

The most important architectural reminder of Venice's long reign *(above)* is now a shop selling museum-grade reproductions of Classical works of art.

7 Municipal Gardens

In the summer months, the gardens host a popular wine festival and are a good place to begin a walk or to escape the intense heat. The remains of an old Muslim cemetery here were covered by the gardens in 1924.

8 Inner Harbour

The small inner harbour, below the fortress, is one of the most picturesque in Greece, with ramshackle old houses, small boats at anchor and a busy quayside.

9 Venetian Gate (Porta Guora)

The only remnant of the city's Venetian fortifications is an arched stone gate, leading from the picturesque old quarter into the modern part of the city. Other gates were dismantled to provide better vehicle access.

10 Beach

Rethymno's town beach *(above)* starts just east of the main harbour breakwater and stretches eastward. Behind it is an esplanade lined with palm trees planted in the 1990s, and an almost continuous chain of open-air cafés and restaurants.

Muslims and Hajis

Rethymno's many Turkish features hint at a multi-ethnic past. Until Crete's independence in 1908, the town had a large Turkish Muslim population. Many later moved to Rhodes, which was then still under Turkish rule. The common Cretan name prefix "Hadzi" is a reminder of that era, originally indicating a Cretan who had made the pilgrimage ("Haj" in Turkish/Arabic) to the Holy Land.

Gortys

The ruins of Gortys, in the middle of the fertile Messara plain, date from a much later era than Crete's Minoan palaces. The large site, surrounded by trees, is less crowded than Crete's other top archaeological attractions, though it is just as impressive. It was probably first settled by the Minoans, but flourished later during the period of the Dorian city-states in the 6th century BC. In the 2nd century BC, Gortys defeated its rival Phaestos to become the leading Cretan city.

2 Roman Odeion and Code of Laws

Built into the walls of a Roman odeion are stone slabs inscribed with a code of laws *(above)*, dating from about 500 BC. This is regarded as Gortys' most significant archaeological feature.

The Nymphaeum

🐟 To combine your visit to Gortys with an afternoon swim or an overnight stop, drive to Matala, 30 km (20 miles) east of Gortys, which has a fine sandy beach.

🍴 Instead of using the rather spartan on-site cafeteria at Gortys, head for the nearby village of Agioi Deka, where there are several pleasant tavernas and a historic church.

Map J5 • 1 km (half a mile) from Agioi Deka • 28920 31144 • Summer: 8am–8pm daily; winter: 8am–3pm daily • Closed some national holidays • Adm €4; concessions €2

1 Basilica of Agios Titos

The impressive remains of the tree-aisled basilica *(above)* indicate that Christianity was already well established on the island by the 5th century, when the basilica was built. It is named after St Titus (Agios Titos), who accompanied St Paul the Apostle to Crete in AD 59 and became the first bishop of Crete.

3 Praetorium

A courtyard and stumps of marble columns *(above)* are all that remain of the palace of the Roman governor of Crete and Libya.

4 Temple of Pythian Apollo

Built in the 7th century BC, the temple had a monumental altar added in the Hellenistic period and was converted into a Christian church in the 2nd century AD.

Roman Baths
Remnants of the baths, which would have been a social hub of the Roman city, can be seen among olive groves south of the Praetorium.

Temple of Isis and Serapis
Ancient Crete had links with ancient Egypt, as shown by the remains of this temple dedicated to the Egyptian deities.

Museum
A collection of marble statuary unearthed at Gortys is on display in a small pavilion on the site, though many of the more impressive finds are held at the Irakleio Archaeological Museum *(see pp14–15)*. The on-site collection includes images of gods, emperors and Roman notables *(above)*.

Plan of the site

Roman Amphitheatre
The Roman amphitheatre *(above)* is surprisingly small for a settlement as important as Roman Gortys, but its tiers of stone seats are well preserved and it is easy to imagine it in use as a venue for drama, oratory or gladiatorial combat.

Roman Agora
An impressive statue of the god of healing, Asklepios (now in Irakleio Archaeological Museum), was discovered at the Roman Agora. The agora, or marketplace, was the heart of any ancient Greco-Roman city.

Acropolis (Kastro)
Outside the main site, formidable Roman ramparts *(below)* and a small tower, known as the Kastro ("castle") stand guard on a low hilltop. The site is fenced, and the worn-out path makes access difficult.

Byzantine Gortys
After the Roman conquest of 65 BC, Gortys became capital of the Roman province of Crete and Cyrene (modern Libya). It continued to flourish as an important Byzantine provincial hub until, with the weakening of the Byzantine empire, it was sacked by Saracen invaders in the late 7th century AD. It was finally abandoned by its inhabitants in 824.

TOP 10 Samaria Gorge

The Samaria Gorge, which cuts its way through the Lefka Ori (White Mountains) from the Omalos Plateau to the Libyan Sea, is one of the most striking areas of natural beauty in Greece. Peaks soar on both sides of the gorge, flanked by pine woods and wildflower meadows. Beginning 1,250 m (4,100 ft) above sea level, it emerges on the coast close to the little village of Agia Roumeli after passing through the narrow Sideresportes or "Iron Gates".

Wild goat

🐾 Though fit walkers can complete the 17-km (11-mile) trek in about five hours, it is best to allow eight, including a break of at least an hour. Rest in the hottest part of the day in summer.

🥤 Take plenty of water – at least one litre per person. There are designated rest areas where you can picnic in the shade, and at Agia Roumeli, there are small tavernas for your recuperation.

• Map C4 • Gorge open May–mid-Oct (weather permitting – phone first to check) 7am–8pm daily
• Forest Guardhouse, Xyloskalo 28210 67179
• Forest Guardhouse, Agia Roumeli 28250 91254 • Adm €5
• Keep your date-stamped ticket, which you must hand in at the Agia Roumeli gate as you leave

Top 10 Sights

1. Xyloskalo
2. Gigilos and Volakia Peaks
3. Neroutsiko – Riza Sikias
4. Church of Agios Nikolaos
5. Samaria
6. Osia Maria
7. Sideresportes
8. Tarra (Old Agia Roumeli)
9. New Agia Roumeli
10. Agios Pavlos Beach

1 Xyloskalo

The zig-zag path down through the gorge is called the Xyloskalo. The toughest part plummets a breathtaking 1,000 m (3,300 ft) in little more than 2 km (1 mile), passing through pine and cypress woods along the way.

2 Gigilos and Volakia Peaks

Above the Xyloskalo to the west, the skyline is dominated by the massive peaks of Gingilos and Volakia. These mountaintops may remain snow covered well into early summer when the temperatures at sea level are scorching.

3 Neroutsiko and Riza Sikias

The springs of Neroutsiko and Riza Sikias meet at the foot of the Xyloskalo. In winter, they form a fierce torrent that makes the gorge impassable, but in summer, they dry to a trickle.

4 Church of Agios Nikolaos

Not far from the foot of the Xyloskalo and the springs, the tiny, roughly built chapel of Agios Nikolaos stands in the shade of pine and cypress trees, next to an official rest area.

5 Samaria
The last dwellers in the gorge abandoned this village in 1962 when the area was designated a national park. The ghostly cottages have become ever more derelict.

6 Osia Maria
Dwarfed by steep cliffs, the small church of Osia Maria contains 14th-century frescoes and lends its name to the village of Samaria and to the gorge itself.

Plan of the Gorge

7 Sideresportes
Near the shrine of Afendis Christos, the gorge narrows to just 3 m (9 ft) of space separating rocky walls that rise 700 m (over 2,000 ft).

8 Tarra (Old Agia Roumeli)
A crumbling Turkish fort, a ruined Venetian church and a few tumbledown cottages are all that remain of the old village of Agia Roumeli. Below these ruins lies the site of the small Hellenistic city state of Tarra.

9 New Agia Roumeli
The inhabitants of Agia Roumeli abandoned their village in the 1960s, intent on a new location by the sea. The new village has since grown into a cheerful string of tavernas and guesthouses spread out along a single street.

Getting Around
Several tour companies run daily escorted walks, which include transport to and from the gorge. There are also regular buses from Chania to Omalos, 1 km (half a mile) from Xyloskalo. Independent walkers must report to the Forest Guardhouse at Xyloskalo before setting out. There are many guesthouses in Agia Roumeli, and while no roads service this stretch of coast, ferries run daily to Chora Sfakion and Sougia.

10 Agios Pavlos Beach
Just east of Agia Roumeli, Agios Pavlos beach is a long, uncrowded stretch of pebbles. It is named after the tiny chapel here dedicated to St Paul.

⟋10 The Amari Valley and Mt Idi

The remote Amari Valley, overlooked by the summit of Mt Idi, is one of the most scenic regions in Crete, dotted with tiny village churches – some of them more than 700 years old – and olive groves and vineyards. This upland region is surprisingly fertile, thanks to topsoil washed from the surrounding slopes, and in the Byzantine era was among the wealthiest regions in Crete. A heartland of the Cretan resistance struggle in World War II, many of its villages were destroyed by the Germans in retaliation for attacks by Cretan guerrillas.

Fresco at Agia Anna, near Amari village

Panagia at Thronas

🌀 Amari is the best base for exploring the valley and surrounding mountains on foot. There are several tavernas, rooms to rent and a post office where you can change money.

Guided fossil-hunting and herb-gathering walks (€30 per person) around the Amari Valley are organized by Lamvros Papoutsakis in Thronos village (28330 22760). Another walk takes participants to the Psiloritis summit at dawn (€50 per person).

Map G–H4 • Greek National Tourism Organization, Sofokli Venizelou, Rethymno • 28310 29148

Top 10 Sights

1. Mt Idi (Psiloritis) Summit
2. Idaian Cave
3. Amari Village
4. Kamares Cave
5. Hromonastiri
6. The Memorial to Peace
7. Thronos
8. Moni Asomaton
9. Agios Ioannis Theologos
10. Fourfouras

1 Mt Idi (Psiloritis) Summit

Towering above the remote valley, the 2,456-m (8,060-ft) peak of Mt Idi, also called Ida and Psiloritis, is the highest mountain in Crete. Marked walking trails *(see p53)* lead to the summit from the Nida Plateau, 23 km (14 miles) by road from Anogeia village.

2 Idaian Cave

According to Greek myth, Zeus, chief of the Olympian gods, was raised in this enormous cavern *(below)*, 20 minutes' walk from the Nida Plateau. In ancient times, this was a

place of pilgrimage. Artifacts such as bronze shields, which were left as offerings to Zeus in the 8th century BC, are in the Irakleio Archaeological Museum. The cavern is open daily.

Amari Village
A Venetian clock tower *(right)* on the main square is one of the older buildings in the valley. Just outside the village, some of Crete's oldest Christian frescoes, dated 1225, are in Agia Anna church.

Kamares Cave
This cave, where remarkable Minoan pottery known as Kamares ware was discovered, is a four-hour trek from Kamares village. This sacred site was dedicated to the goddess Eileithyia.

Hromonastiri
The church of Agios Efstathio, outside the village of Hromonastiri, contains faded frescoes, dating from the 11th century, which may be the oldest of their kind in Crete.

The Memorial to Peace
German artist Karen Raeck's work, to the north of the Nida Plateau, is a winged figure outlined in huge natural stone boulders *(above)*.

Thronos
The 14th-century church of the Panagia at Thronos contains striking frescoes and traces of ancient mosaics. Nearby are the ruins of a Hellenistic city, Sivritis.

Moni Asomaton
The monastery of Asomaton *(left)*, built in the Venetian era, is now deserted and spooky. It stands in a fertile oasis of plane trees, palms and eucalyptus.

Agios Ioannis Theologos
The church of St John the Divine, built in the 13th century, stands by the road just north of Kardaki village. The fine frescoes were painted in 1347.

Fourfouras
A pretty village set in stunning mountain scenery, Fourfouras is one of the jumping-off spots for the ascent of Mt Idi and some of the less challenging hikes on the Psiloritis massif.

Getting Around the Valley
Though the Amari Valley feels remote, there is one bus daily Monday–Friday from Rethymno to the two largest villages, Thronos and Amari. With a hired car, it is possible to drive up one side of the valley and down the other. Of the two roads, the eastern route is the most spectacular.

Gournia

Unearthed by the American archaeologist Harriet Boyd Hawes between 1901 and 1904, Gournia is the best preserved Minoan town in Crete, though it receives few visitors. Its layout, with narrow stepped streets and tiny houses, is surprisingly similar to that of Cretan villages to this day. It is also one of the oldest sites, inhabited from around 3000 BC, though the surviving buildings date from the later Second Palace Period. Like other Minoan settlements, it was destroyed by earthquake and fire around 1450 BC. The honeycomb of ruins stands only waist high.

Stairway

Remains of workshops

🕐 Unfortunately, the beaches near Gournia (like most along this stretch of coast) are dirty and unappealing.

🍴 There is nowhere to eat at Gournia. Pachia Ammos, 3 km (2 miles) east, has a string of restaurants on its waterfront.

Map N5 • South of coast road, 18 km (11 miles) east of Agios Nikolaos • 28420 93028 • 8am–3pm Tue–Sun • Adm €2

Top 10 Sights

1. Courtyard
2. Stairway
3. Central Palace Court
4. Palace
5. Storerooms
6. Shrine
7. Carpenter's Workshop
8. Potter's Workshop
9. Bronzesmith's Workshop
10. Wash Basins

Courtyard
At the southern end of the site, an expansive courtyard *(below)* would have been the hub of the settlement and may have been the town's market. It was probably also used for ceremonial purposes.

Stairway
The L-shaped stair that rises from the courtyard to the central court of the palace is characteristic of Minoan palaces. The design of it echoes similar ceremonial stairs found in virtually every Minoan palace site in Crete.

Central Palace Court
Access to the central court of the palace from the courtyard below is by the ceremonial staircase. The Minoan ruler of Gournia may well have used this antechamber to the small palace building *(below)* as his audience hall.

Palace

The palace, which may have been the dwelling place of a governor who ruled Gournia on behalf of the Minoan ruler of Knosos, is a miniature version of the more important Minoan royal palaces. In the centre of the palace is a sacrificial altar.

Storerooms

Adjoining the palace are storerooms (left), or magazines, where grain, oil and other essentials would have been kept in earthenware jars.

Plan of the site

Shrine

A cobbled, mosaic-decorated path leads steeply up to a small shrine, which was found to contain cult objects. The terracotta goddess figurines and snake are now displayed in the Irakleio Archaeological Museum (see pp14–15).

Carpenter's Workshop

Gournia was clearly a thriving, self-contained community, and tools and other materials found in this small building indicate that it was used by a woodworker who may also have lived on the premises with his family.

Potter's Workshop

Clay fragments indicate this was a potter's workshop (right). The finds unearthed in this and other buildings indicate Gournia was suddenly abandoned rather than slowly run down.

Bronzesmith's Workshop

Bronze nails and scraps, and a simple stone anvil suggest a smithy used in smelting bronze. Tools, weapons, utensils and votive objects from Gournia are at Irakleio Archaeological Museum.

Wash Basins

The crude stone washing basins found outside almost every building in Gournia are known as *gournes* in modern Greek. They gave their name to the long lost site when it was rediscovered.

Lost Names

Although some Minoan scripts have been deciphered, archaeologists still have no way of knowing what the Minoans called most of their cities. The names by which they are known today stem from words used by the much later Greek settlers who occupied the island long after the collapse of Minoan civilization.

Left **Turkish and Egyptian forces in 1896** Right **Venetian fortress**

10 **Moments in History**

1 1750 BC: Golden Age of Minoan Culture

Crete is the centre of the Minoan civilization, which is marked by the building of Knosos and other palaces. Mycenaeans take over Knosos in 1450 BC.

2 Roman Conquest

The first Roman invasion of Crete in 71 BC is repulsed by the Dorian Greeks, but a second attack in 69 BC succeeds. Some Cretan cities side with the invaders, and by 67 BC, Crete is firmly in Roman hands.

Cretan statue of Hadrian

3 Byzantine Reconquest

The Byzantine Empire loses Crete to Arab invaders in AD 824. The Emperor Nicephoros Phokas reconquers the island in 961.

4 Venetian Rule

Crete falls into Venetian hands after 1204, when the Fourth Crusade goes awry and the Byzantine Emperor is deposed by an army of Frankish crusaders in alliance with Venice. Cretans rebel against the Venetians, but without success.

5 The Turks

Chania and Rethymno quickly fall to an attack by Turks in 1645. Venetian sea-power enables the Venetian capital of Candia (modern Irakleio) to resist a 21-year siege, but Venice finally surrenders in 1669. The Cretans rise too against the Turks. The first major rebellion begins in 1770 in mountainous Sfakia and is led by Ioannis Daskalogiannis. It ends badly, however, with Sfakia conquered.

6 War of Independence

In 1821, a nationwide rising in mainland Greece flares into a full-scale and eventually successful War of Independence. In Crete, Chatzimichalis Dalianis

Painting by Jan Peeters, said to be of the Siege of Candia in the 17th century

German troops in 1941

and fewer than 400 rebels raise the Greek banner at Frangokastello, where they are besieged and slaughtered. Crete remains under the Turkish yoke.

7 1866: Another Rebellion Against Turks

Undaunted by these heroic failures, Crete rises again in 1866, with a self-appointed Cretan Assembly declaring independence and union with Greece. The Turks bring in Egyptian troops to quell the rebels, but in Europe there is growing sympathy for the Cretan cause.

8 Great Powers Intervene

Several risings in the last decades of the 19th century culminate in the landing of Greek troops in 1897 and international intervention.

9 Union with Greece

In 1905, Eleftherios Venizelos – a minister in Prince George's governorship of Crete – calls for a nationalist revolution and in 1908, the Cretan Assembly declares union *(enosis)* with Greece.

10 Occupation and Liberation in World War II

German forces drive the Allies out of Crete in May 1941, but Cretan guerrillas continue to resist. Most German troops flee Greece in autumn 1944 as Allied troops land, but the garrison at Chania holds out until the end of the war in May 1945.

Top 10 Empires and Governments

1 Minoan Empires
The Minoan civilization emerged between 3000 and 1900 BC. A volcanic explosion may have destroyed the Minoan cities around 1450 BC.

2 Mycenaeans
Myceanean Greeks from the mainland settled in Crete after 1450 BC.

3 The Dorians
Dorian Greeks from northern Greece arrived in the 12th century BC, driving the descendants of the Minoans into remote areas.

4 Dorian City States
Gortys and Kidonia (modern Chania) were among the most powerful.

5 Roman Empire
Gortys (which had sided with Rome) became capital of the province of Crete and Cyrene (modern Libya).

6 Byzantine Empire
In the 4th century AD Crete became part of the Byzantine realm.

7 Arab Conquest
In AD 824–961, Arab forces led by the Saracen ruler of Andalucia, Abu Hafs, overturned Crete.

8 Venetian Empire
In 1204, the Republic of Venice took control of Crete and the Aegean islands.

9 Ottoman Empire
The Ottoman Turks invaded Crete in strength in 1645 and held the island until the end of the 19th century.

10 Kingdom of the Hellenes
Crete was united with Greece in 1913. In 1923, 30,000 Muslim Cretans were expelled from Crete.

Left **Bull fresco, Knosos** Right **Gortys**

Ancient Sites

1 Knosos
Just outside Irakleio, Knosos is by far the most striking of the ancient Minoan palace ruins on Crete. Dating back more than 3,500 years, it was destroyed, probably by a volcanic eruption, around 1450 BC and not redis-covered until the late 19th century *(see pp8–11)*.

2 Phaestos
The ruins of the Minoan palace at Phaes-tos, on a hilltop by the south coast of Crete, are second only to those at Knosos. A maze of walls and courtyards marks the site of the Second Palace at Phaestos, built around 1600 BC. Hieroglyphics on the clay Phaestos Disc still puzzle scientists *(see pp20–21)*.

3 Gortys
The ruined city of Gortys, with basilica and remnants of a Roman provincial governor's palace, dates from the early Christian era. The site extends over a wide area, and is usually uncrowded, so it can be explored at leisure *(see pp24–5)*.

4 Gournia
The well-preserved Minoan town of Gournia, a maze of roofless stone walls, makes an interesting contrast with the better-known Minoan palac-es. This was a working community, and archaeol-ogists discovered work-shops used by potters, smiths and carpenters alongside tiny houses surrounding a small palace *(see pp30–31)*.

Giant pot, Malia

5 Agia Triada
A treasury of Minoan relics, including tablets inscribed with the still undeciphered Minoan Linear A script, has been discovered on this site of a Minoan villa, built about 1700 BC. The site was later occupied by Mycenaean settlers, who built a *megaron* (chief's hall) and a village with a unique row of porticoed shops *(see p81)*.

6 Malia
East of the busy summer holiday resort of Malia is an archaeological site of the same name. The Minoan double-axe symbol, or

Phaestos

Left **Agia Triada** Right **Malia Archaeological Site**

labrys, is carved into two pillars of a small shrine, which forms part of the remains of a palace dating circa 1600 BC. Excavations are still going on near the palace site. ✆ *3 km (2 miles) east of Malia • Map M4 • 28970 31597 • 8am–5pm Tue–Sun • Adm*

Zakros

The fourth largest of Crete's Minoan palaces, Zakros was rediscovered in 1961 by Cretan archaeologist Nikolaos Platon. The site had not been plundered, and finds included a stunning rock crystal jug, now in the Irakleio Archaeological Museum *(see pp14–15)*. Remains of the palace and a cistern can be seen. ✆ *Kato Zakros • Map R5 • 28430 26897 • 8am–6pm daily • Adm*

Praisos

This scenic site – with only the remnants of a temple, house foundations and a city wall to be seen – was the last enclave of the Eteocretan ("true Cretan") descendants of the Minoans. It survived until the 2nd century BC. ✆ *By Nea Praisos village • Map Q5 • Unenclosed • Free*

Itanos

The remains of a Hellenistic wall, foundations of two early Christian basilicas, and toppled walls and columns are the only indications that this was once an important city. It flourished until early medieval times, when it was destroyed by Saracen raiders. ✆ *2 km (1 mile) north of Vai • Map R4 • Unenclosed • Free*

Levin

Ancient Levin, on a hilltop just outside the modern village of Lendas, is now no more than a scattering of ruined walls and pillars around a stone arch. The site was a sanctuary dedicated to Asklepios, the god of healing. From the 3rd century BC to the Christian era, it was an important place of pilgrimage. ✆ *North of Lendas • Map J6 • Unenclosed • Free*

Zakros Palace

Left **Chania Museum** Centre **Siteia Museum** Right **Byzantine Collection of Chania**

Art and Archaeological Museums

1 Irakleio Archaeological Museum

The largest museum in Crete, and well worth visiting. In addition to exhibits from Crete, the collection includes significant finds from Greece *(see pp14–15)*.

2 Chania Archaeological Museum

Housed in a historic building which was first a Venetian church then a Turkish mosque, the museum is packed with Minoan finds, Hellenistic and Roman marble sculpture, pottery and jewellery found at archaeological sites in western Crete. § *Map D2*
• *28210 90334* • *8am–3pm Tue–Sun*
• *Disabled access* • *Adm*

3 Siteia Archaeological Museum

The most important exhibits are from the palace site at Zakros, on Crete's east coast, which was uncovered in 1961. They include clay tablets inscribed with the symbols of the Minoan Linear A

script, as well as bronze tools and kitchen utensils. § *Map Q4* • *Fiskokefalou 3* • *28430 23917* • *8am–3pm Tue–Sun* • *Adm*

Statue from Rethymno Archaeological Museum

4 Rethymno Archaeological Museum

In a converted bastion built by the Turks, the collection extends from the Stone Age to the Minoan and Hellenistic eras, with finds from archaeological sites, caves and cemeteries in the Rethymno region. Among the highlights are late Minoan burial caskets, or *larnakes*, and burial goods found in Minoan cemetery sites. § *Map Q1*
• *Himaras, Fortetza* • *28310 54668*
• *8am–3pm Tue–Sun* • *Adm*

5 Byzantine Collection of Chania

The fine collection of beautiful Cretan icons is the best reason to visit this small museum next to Chania's harbour fortress. The collection spans 1,000 years of Byzantine history and sheds light on an often ignored chapter in Crete's complex history. § *Map D2*
• *82 Theotokopoulou* • *28210 96046*
• *8am–3pm Tue–Sun* • *Adm*

6 Archaeological Museum of Kissamos

Housed in a fine Venetian-Turkish building, this museum offers finds from sites such as Polyrinia and Falasarna in the far west of Crete. Most of the artifacts are from the

Gardens, Irakleio Archaeological Museum

Hellenestic or Roman period, and include jewellery, statues and a wonderful mosaic floor. 🔊 *Map B2*
• *Tzanaki Square* • *28220 83308*
• *8:30am–3pm Tue–Sun* • *Adm*

7 Museum of Contemporary Art, Rethymno

This museum has around 500 works by the artist L. Kanakakis, as well as works by other leading, contemporary Greek artists. The pieces range from the 1950s to the present day. It also holds temporary exhibitions, as well as classes and workshops, open to the public. 🔊 *Map Q1 • Himaras 5, Rethymno 74100 • 28310 52530 • May–Oct: 9am–2pm & 7–9pm Tue–Fri, 10am–3pm Sat & Sun; Nov–Apr: 9am–2pm Tue–Fri, 6–9pm Wed & Fri, 10am–3pm Sat & Sun • Adm*

8 Ierapetra Archaeological Museum

Exhibits include huge clay storage jars *(pithoi)*, Minoan sarcophagi made of clay *(larnakes)* statues, and bronze weapons and tools dating from the time of the Dorian city-states, when Ierapetra became one of the most powerful cities in eastern Crete. 🔊 *Map N6*
• *1 Kostoula Adrianou Ierapetra • 28420 28721 • 9am–3pm Tue–Sun • Adm*

9 Archanes Collection

Finds from the Minoan cemetery discovered at Fourni, just north of Archanes village,

Archanes Archaeological Museum

are displayed in the village's small archaeological museum along with relics from other nearby sites. 🔊 *Map K4 • Kalochristianaki, Archanes • 28107 52712 • Summer: 8am–3pm Wed–Mon • Free*

10 El Greco Museum

Copies of paintings and biographical material relating to the life of the Cretan-born artist Domenikos Theotokopoulos, better known as El Greco, are displayed in a restored Venetian building in Fodele village, which is claimed to be his birthplace.
🔊 *Map J3 • Fodele village, just south of main coast road • 28105 21500*
• *Summer: 9am–7pm daily • Adm*

El Greco Museum

Left **Cretan weaving** Right **Gavalochori Historical Museum**

Folklore Museums

1 Lychnostatis Open Air Museum of Folk Culture

Traditional Cretan ways of life that lasted for centuries only began to die out in recent decades. This open-air museum gives some insight into life on the island before tourism, TVs and mobile phones. Exhibits include a windmill and an old stone cottage. ⊗ *Chersonisos • Map L4 • 28970 23660 • Apr–Nov: 9am–2pm Sun–Fri; winter: visits by appt • Adm • www.lychnostatis.gr*

Lychnostatis Open Air Museum

2 Historical and Folk Art Museum, Rethymno

A small museum housed in a Venetian mansion displays relics of a vanished way of life, including colourful woven artifacts, lace, silver jewellery and ceramics. ⊗ *Vernardou 30 • Map F3 • 28310 23398 • 9:30am–2pm Mon–Sat • Adm*

3 War Museum of Askifou

This fascinating museum, located in the tiny village of Askifou, was founded by George Hatzidakis. He wanted to collect every vestige of the Cretan struggle between

Historical and Folk Art Museum, Rethymno

1941–44. Today, the collection has over 2,000 items. ⊗ *Askifou • Map E4 • 69791 49719 • 8am–8pm daily • Free but donations welcome • www.warmuseumaskifou.com*

4 Museum of Cretan Ethnology, Vori

Excellent collection which gives real insight into the hard life of Cretan villagers in years gone by. For example, there are displays on how wild foods – from dandelions to snails – featured in their diet! ⊗ *Vori • Map H5 • 28920 91110 • Apr–Oct: 11am–5pm daily; closed winter except for groups by appt • Adm*

5 Museum Papa Michalis Georgoulakis, Asomatos

The late priest Papa Michalis began his collection at age 15. This museum houses an eclectic range of items illustrating Cretan life in the last century. ⊗ *Asomatos • Map F4 • 28320 31674 • Summer: 10am–5pm Mon–Sat, 10am–3pm Sun • Adm*

6 Agios Nikolaos Folklore Museum

Overlooking Agios Nikolaos's lagoon-like inner harbour, the Folklore Museum houses colourful textiles and costumes, plus farming and fishing equipment. ⊗ *Kondilaki 2 • Map N4 • 28410 25093 • May–Oct: 10am–2pm daily • Adm*

7 Arolithos Museum of Agricultural History and Popular Art

This museum is linked with a holiday village which tries to give its

guests a taste of traditional Cretan life, with craft workers who use traditional methods, a restaurant and bakery with wood-burning ovens, and live music and dancing in the evening. ✪ *Arolithos village, 8 km west of Irakleio on old highway • Map J4 • 28108 21050 • Apr–Oct: 9am–3pm, Nov–Mar: visits by appt • Adm • www.arolithos.com*

8 Cretan House Folklore Museum, Chania

Traditional looms and spinning wheels, richly coloured rugs, wall hangings and embroidery can be found at this delightful place. ✪ *46B Chalidon • Map D2 • 28210 90816 • 9am–7pm Mon–Sat • Adm*

9 Folklore and Martial Museum, Somatas

A quirky, two-room museum with a collection of farm tools, early radios and household items in one room, and weapons, medals, uniforms and memorabilia from World War II in the other. Opening hours can be erratic. ✪ *Somatas, Rethymno • Map F3 • 28310 41315 • 9am–6pm daily • Free but donations welcomed*

10 Historical and Folklore Museum of Gavalochori

This excellent small museum is housed in an old Venetian-Turkish mansion and depicts the history and culture of the village. Highlights include local skills such as silk spinning, masonry and carpentry. ✪ *Gavalochori village • Map E3 • 28250 23222 • 10am–8pm Mon–Sat, 11am–6pm Sun • Adm*

Cretan House Folklore Museum, Chania

Traditional Crafts

1 Weaving
Traditional hand looms are still in use, made by skilled craftsmen from cypress, walnut or mulberry wood.

2 Embroidery
Rethymno was a major centre for embroidery, a skill introduced to Crete in the Byzantine era.

3 Spinning
Older village women still spin wool into yarn using a spindle and distaff – a skill that hasn't changed since the time of the Minoans.

4 Musical Instruments
Crete has a strong tradition of making musical instruments *(see pp60–61)* and many places still make the *lyra*, a three-stringed violin, and the *laouta* (mandolin).

5 Church Embroidery
Crete's Orthodox monks and nuns embellish sumptuous church vestments with gold, silver and silk stitching.

6 Wood Carving
Olive, cypress and mulberry yield a hard wood loved by skilled Cretan carpenters.

7 Leatherwork
Everything from shepherds' boots and mule harnesses to satchels, handbags and sheepskin garments.

8 Silversmithing
Silver jewellery and religious objects such as icon frames and crucifixes.

9 Lace
Silk *kopaneli* lace is made by bobbin weaving, a skill revived in Gavalochori.

10 Antique Weapons
The Cretan *pallikar* (warrior-hero) loved highly decorated weapons. Authentic antique weapons are highly valued.

Left **Rethymno** Centre **Spinalonga** Right **Aptera**

TOP 10 Venetian and Turkish Castles

1 Rethymno
The massive fortress that dominates Rethymno's harbour was built by the Venetians with sloping walls to better deflect the Ottoman Empire's gigantic cannon. But it proved no match for the military ingenuity of the Turks, and fell after a short siege. Ironically, it became a far more successful stronghold for the Turkish Ottomans *(see also p22).*

2 Frangokastello
The Venetians built this romantic coastal fortress to defend the south coast from Saracen pirates. In 1821, it was occupied by a small force of Cretan rebels, holding out against a vastly greater Turkish army. The rebels were defeated of course, but, according to legend, once a year their ghosts appear from the sea to reclaim the ruined castle *(see p59 & p92).* ❧ Map E4

Frangokastello bust

3 Spinalonga
A formidable island fortress built in 1579 to command the entrance to the Gulf of Mirabello. Venice managed to hang on to it even after the surrender of Candia (Irakleio) in 1669, and gave it up only by treaty in 1715. After Turkish withdrawal, it was used for a time as a leper colony *(see pp104–105).*

4 Chania
The Venetians lost Chania to their arch-rivals, the Genoese, in 1263. They regained it 22 years later, and set about making the town impregnable, starting with walls around the hill above the harbour in the district still known as Kastelli (the castle). Further walls followed, but though they may have deterred occasional pirate raids, they proved ineffective when the Turks assailed the city in 1645. ❧ Map D2

Frangokastello

Paleochora

Kastel Selinou, as Paleochora was first known, was built in 1279 to guard the southwest against pirates. The great Turkish corsair Barbarossa destroyed it in 1539. The Turks saw no need to rebuild it, and it has remained an elegant ruin ever since. ✎ *Map B4*

Venetian Acropolis and Polyrinia

On a hilltop above Paleokastro, a Venetian keep shares the peak with the ruins of the Hellenistic city of Polyrinia, which thrived until the Saracen invasion of the 9th century. Stone from Hellenistic buildings, already 1,000 years old when the Venetians arrived, seems to have been incorporated into the castle walls. ✎ *Map B2*

Aptera

Climb the bastions of the Aptera Fort, on a hilltop near the ruins of Byzantine Aptera for sweeping views. Below, across the coastal highway, is the grim Itzedin Fort, now under restoration and due to become a summer concert venue. ✎ *Map D2*

Da Molini Castle Ruins, Alikianos

Though much overgrown, the dilapidated walls standing among orange and lemon trees are still impressive. The castle was the scene of a famous massacre, when the

Siteia's Venetian Fortress

Cretan rebel leader Georgios Kandanoleon was betrayed by Francesco Molini during his wedding to Molini's daughter. ✎ *Map C2*

Venetian Fortress, Siteia

Siteia's restored Venetian fort is used as an open-air theatre for concerts and plays in summer. The fortress is all that remains of the city's once substantial ring of battlements which resisted a three-year siege by the Turks in 1648–51. ✎ *Map Q4*

Venetian Tower, Finikas, Loutro

The lonely tower, standing on a headland between Loutro and the bay of Finix, is yet another Venetian relic. Nearby are a few scattered blocks, the remains of a Byzantine church and also a Hellenistic town, the latter an important seaport when the Romans ruled Crete. ✎ *Map D4*

Left **Panagia Kera** Centre **Moni Arkadiou** Right **Moni Agia Triada**

Churches and Monasteries

1 Moni Arkadiou

Though founded in the 5th century, most of the monastic buildings here date from the 16th century. Moni Arkadiou has a special significance for Cretans. During the great revolt of 1866, the monastery – crowded with refugees as well as Cretan freedom fighters – was besieged by the Turks. Rather than surrender, the rebel defenders blew up their gunpowder stores, killing themselves and many of their enemies. ✆ *Map G4 • 28310 83076 • 9am–8pm daily • Adm*

2 Panagia Kera

The most important Byzantine-era church in Crete, Panagia Kera, was built in the 13th and 14th centuries. The church is dedicated to the Virgin and to saints Anthony and Anna, and is adorned with expressive murals depicting the two saints, as well as 14 scenes portraying the secret life of the Virgin Mary after Christ's Crucifixion and Resurrection. ✆ *Map N5 • 28410 51525 • 8am–3pm Tue–Sun • Adm*

3 Moni Toplou

The Toplou monastery's forbidding exterior is deceptive, for like many Greek monasteries it was fortified against bandits during the Middle Ages. Inside, however, is a different world of serene, flower-filled courtyards

and cloisters, and a church that houses one of the greatest Cretan works of religious art, the icon *Lord, Thou Art Great* by Ioannis Kornaros. ✆ *Map Q4 • 28430 61226 • 9am–1pm, 2–6pm daily • Adm*

4 Moni Agia Triada

The Monastery of the Holy Trinity stands among its own olive groves, and although its monastic community has dwindled to just a few members, its lovely old buildings are gradually being restored. Visitors are welcome, and the monks will happily sell you some of their home-grown olive oil, which is of high quality. ✆ *Map D2 • 28210 63572 • 9am–7pm daily (Museum Hall closed Sun) • Adm*

5 Moni Gouverneto

Only three elderly monks remain in this isolated monastery, deep in the wilds of the bleak and barren Akrotiri Peninsula. The building encloses a tranquil courtyard, in which stands a small chapel with some of the oldest frescoes in Crete. ✆ *Map D2 • 28210 63319 • 9am–noon & 5–7pm Mon, Tue & Thu; 9am–noon & 5–8pm Sat; 5–11am, 5–8pm Sun • Adm*

6 Moni Preveli

Built during the 17th century to replace a more remote monastery building, Moni Preveli's peaceful

Moni Toplou

Moni Preveli

dormitories and cloisters look inward, onto an 18th-century courtyard with a 19th-century church and a small museum. Exhibits include lavishly ornamented vestments, church silver and icons. ◈ *Map F5 • 28320 31246 • 9am–8:30pm daily • Adm*

Agioi Deka Church
This 13th-century Byzantine Church of the Ten Saints stands on the spot where ten Cretan Christians were martyred by the troops of the Roman Emperor Decius in AD 250. A striking icon depicting the ten saints with golden halos is displayed in the nave. ◈ *Map J5 • 8am–5pm • Free*

Moni Chrissopygis
The Convent of the Source of Life, like so many Cretan monasteries, looks more like a castle than a religious dwelling. It is relatively new, built in 1863, and has a studio in which icons

are painted using age-old techniques. ◈ *Map C2 • 28210 91125 • 8am–noon & 3:30–6pm daily • Adm*

Moni Katholikou
In a rugged valley riddled with caves once used by hermits, the abandoned monastery of Gouverneto is a ghostly place, with crumbling buildings that seem to have grown out of the rockface. ◈ *Map D2 • Open access*

Agios Nikolaos
This church has a history that reflects Chania's past. It was built by the Venetians, converted into a mosque after the Turkish conquest, and in the early 20th century, converted again into a Greek Orthodox church dedicated to St Nicholas. Its minaret is a relic from the centuries of Muslim worship here. ◈ *Map D2 • 8am–7pm daily • Free*

Moni Chrissopygis

Left **Plakias** Right **Agia Galini**

Beach Resorts

Georgioupoli

At the mouth of a river, 20 km (13 miles) west of Rethymno, lies Georgioupoli. It's a quiet resort, the hub of the village provided by a taverna- and café-lined square shaded by plane trees. Georgioupoli's hotel and self-catering accommodation is spread out along an expansive sandy beach. ◎ *Map E3*

Cave shrine, Malia

Malia

With its great sandy beach and close proximity to Irakleio International Airport, Malia was destined to become one of the island's liveliest package holiday resorts. In July and August it is thronged, attracting a young crowd with its water sports and after-dark scene. But there are peaceful spots, too. ◎ *Map M4*

Limin Chersonisos

Biggest and busiest of the island's resorts, Limin Chersonisos straddles the north coast highway, a long double strip of hotels, apartment complexes, bars, restaurants, dance clubs and shops. Catering mainly to package holidaymakers, it has now almost merged with the neighbouring resorts of Stalida and Malia. ◎ *Map L3*

Plakias

A huge sweep of clean grey sand draws visitors to this little south-coast resort, but there are even better beaches nearby at Damnoni, which can be reached by boat or on foot. Plakias is one of the island's quieter beach resorts, and its accommodation mostly takes the form of self-catering apartments. ◎ *Map F4*

Matala

Matala's coves of fine golden sand, surrounded by rocky red cliffs harbouring Roman cave-tombs, made the place a magnet for hippy travellers in the 1960s. Its tourism is more orthodox now, but Matala is still pleasantly low-key. A good base for exploring Gortys and Phaestos. ◎ *Map G6*

Limin Chersonisos

Discover more at **www.traveldk.com**

Matala

Bali
A small resort, purpose built around coves on the north coast, Bali comes to life in high season, when its "Paradise Beach" glistens with sunbathing bodies. ◈ Map H3

Agia Galini
This picturesque south-coast fishing village took to tourism in the 1980s. Its pebbly beach (crowded in high season) is on a crescent bay, where a small river flows through a thicket of reeds into the sea. Places to eat and drink abound. ◈ Map G5

Makrygialos
Makrygialos has the best and longest beach in eastern Crete, a swathe of grey sand and shingle beneath pine-covered slopes. The village and its neighbour Analipsi have melded into a single chain of tavernas and guesthouses. ◈ Map P5

Paleochora
On a headland crowned by a dilapidated Venetian castle, Paleochora is part fishing village, part resort. It has a crescent of yellow sand on the west side of the promontory and a longer, less crowded pebbly beach on the east. ◈ Map B4

Siteia
The beach at Siteia stretches for miles east of the town and is backed by a ramshackle strip of hotels, guesthouses and cafés. This quiet port on Crete's north coast seems to have escaped the tourist invasion relatively unscathed. ◈ Map Q4

Siteia

Left **A beachside taverna at Agia Roumeli** Right **Irakleio harbour**

🔟 Islands and Boat Trips

The island fortress of Spinalonga

Elafonisi
With its sandy beach and vivid blue lagoon, the tiny, tropical-looking island of Elafonisi is barely separable from the Crete shoreline. Daily boat trips from Paleochora (May–Sep) take an hour each way *(see also p50)*. ◈ *Map A4*

Spinalonga
The island of Spinalonga is a maze of Venetian battlements. Daily boat trips venture here in summer from Plaka, Elounda and Agios Nikolaos – 5, 20 and 35 minutes respectively *(see p104)*.

Gavdos
Europe's southernmost point, where a few simple guesthouses, tavernas and beaches welcome visitors. Boats sail in summer from Agia Roumeli, Paleochora and Chora Sfakion; journey time around 4 hours. Check times at www.anendyk.gr. ◈ *Map D6*

Paleochora–Agia Roumeli
The boat from Paleochora hugs the rugged south coast, calling in at the lazy port of Sougia, before chugging along to Agia Roumeli, a cheerfully ramshackle village at the foot of the Samaria Gorge. ◈ *Map B–C4*

Agia Roumeli–Chora Sfakion
After marching up and down the Samaria Gorge, your journey can be extended along the coast by hopping on one of several daily boats that potter eastwards. All end up at the small port of Chora Sfakion. ◈ *Map C–E4*

The short stretch of water separating Elafonisi from the Crete shoreline

Threshing corn on Gavdos

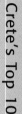

Koufonisi
Coves and sandy beaches attract boats from Makrygialos, while the remains of a Roman amphitheatre attest to a time when the island grew rich from the trade of murex, a sea mollusc from which imperial purple dye was made. ◈ *Map Q6*

Chrysi
Chrysi ("Golden"), so named for its sandy beaches, is known locally as Gaidouronisi ("Donkey Island") because of the Cretan habit of retiring elderly donkeys to uninhabited islands. Daily boat trips from Ierapetra take 30–45 minutes in summer. ◈ *Map N6*

Dia
A group of endangered Cretan wild goats have made their home on Dia. They can be visited on a day trip from Irakleio or Chersonisos. ◈ *Map K3*

Imeri Gramvousa
This island crag just off the Gramvousa peninsula is crowned by a dramatic, crumbling castle. There are several boat trips each week from Kastelli, and excursions through tour agencies in Chania and Rethymno. ◈ *Map B1*

Andikithira
If seeking solitude, this remote island could be an ideal stop-off between Crete and mainland Greece to the northwest. A weekly ferry sails from Rethymno via Kastelli to Andikithira, its larger neighbour Kithira and Gythio on the mainland.

Water Sports

Windsurfing
Boards are readily available for hire, and the best beaches are Georgioupoli, Chersonisos, Malia, Ierapetra and Plakias.

Snorkelling
Crete's crystal waters, teaming with colourful fish, are ideal for snorkelling.

Banana Rides
Inflatable bananas, towed at high speed and carrying up to half a dozen riders, are big in Malia and Chersonisos.

Sea Biscuit Rides
Similarly popular is the "sea biscuit", a tough inflatable ring for a single rider.

Catamaran Sailing
Catamarans can be hired by the hour or day at most resorts, with instruction available for novice sailors.

Yacht Sailing
Yachts can be chartered "bareboat" (without skipper or crew), fully crewed or with a skipper only. The National Tourism Organisation has a list of charter companies.

Scuba Diving
Although archaeological sites and ancient shipwrecks are off-limits, there are good dives to several wrecks from World War II.

Waterskiing
Waterskiing, though expensive, is available at most of the bigger resorts.

Aquapark
At Chersonisos, the Aqua Plus Water Park is a playground of waterslides, waves and waterfalls.

Jet Skiing
Despite the introduction of rules limiting their use, jet skis can still be rented at all major resorts.

Left **Argyroupoli** Centre **Elos** Right **Hamezi**

Villages

1 Kritsa

Sweeping mountain views and a reputation as one of the craft centres of eastern Crete ensures that Kritsa sees its fair share of tourism. Its main street, lined with old stone buildings, is packed with shops selling leather satchels and sandals, embroidery and brightly patterned rugs. Some 30 minutes' walk from Kritsa is the minor archaeological site of Lato, where you can see the remains of a Classical Greek city. ◉ Map M5 • Lato 8:30am–3pm Tue–Sun

2 Argyroupoli

Western Crete's prettiest mountain village is tucked in the foothills of the Lefka Ori, on the site of the Hellenistic town of Lappa. The slopes of its valley setting flourish with lush greenery, watered by natural springs. Argyroupoli makes a good base for relatively easy walking in the surrounding hills. ◉ Map E4

3 Axos

About 10 km (6 miles) inland from the main north coast highway on the way to the scenic Amari Valley, Axos has striking views and an attractive Byzantine church dedicated to Agia Anna. The village is a popular stop for excursion groups, and its tavernas and souvenir shops get crowded around lunch time. On the hillside above Axos are a few scattered remnants of an ancient settlement. ◉ Map H4

4 Kournas

Kournas nestles at the foot of Mt Dafnomadara, in a fertile plain close to Crete's only freshwater lake. Its old stone houses cluster around a steep main street, and the village has two historic Byzantine-Venetian churches, dedicated to Agios Georgios and Agia Irene. ◉ Map E3

5 Topolia

This village, en route from Kastelli to Paleochora, stands amid farm terraces, fields and olive groves, in a well watered

Kournas

Discover more at www.traveldk.com

valley which leads into Kartsomatados Gorge. Its small church of Agia Paraskevi dates from the late Byzantine era. ◈ *Map B3*

Voila

Elos
6 Elos is one of the settlements known as the Enea Choria ("Nine Villages"), which are set among the chestnut forests of the Selloni region. At 1,200 m (3,700 ft) above sea level, it can be pleasantly cooler than the south coast beaches in summer. Surrounded by woodland, Elos has a 14th-century Byzantine chapel and a ruined Turkish aqueduct. ◈ *Map B3*

Alikianos
7 A ruined Venetian castle of the aristocratic Molini family *(see p41)* and a noted 14th-century church of Agios Ioannis (or "Ai-Kir Yanni" in local Cretan dialect) are the prime sights of Alikianos. The village is picturesque in itself, however, and surrounded by citrus groves. ◈ *Map C2*

Hamezi
8 Set above the Bay of Siteia, Hamezi has been inhabited since the Minoan era. Indeed, remnants of Minoan buildings can be seen on a hilltop from the present village, which is a peaceful clutter of whitewashed stone cottages, offset by colourful displays of flowers. ◈ *Map P5*

Voila
9 Voila is Crete's most dramatic ghost village, with lizards scuttling across its ruined walls and crumbling doorways. Voila is overlooked by the tumbledown walls of a Venetian hilltop castle and a Turkish tower, and the only building still intact is the church of Agios Georgios. Surprisingly, two Turkish drinking fountains still provide visitors with fresh water. ◈ *Map Q5*

Ethia
10 It is hard to believe that this desolate hamlet was an important place during Venetian occupation, when it was the fief of the De Mezzo family. Their ruined family tower is now recognized as an important Venetian building, worthy of restoration. ◈ *Map Q5*

Left **Lake Kournas** Right **View from Vai**

TOP 10 Areas of Natural Beauty

1 White Mountains (Lefka Ori)

The White Mountain region of Crete is one of Europe's pocket wildernesses, a region of savage, desert mountains traversed by deep gorges through which small streams flow in spring. The best known of these is the lovely Samaria Gorge *(see pp26–27)*. In winter, the White Mountain peaks are under heavy snow, but in summer temperatures can rise to 35°C. ◈ *Map C–D4*

Windmill, Lasithi Plateau

2 Lasithi

It is still promoted to tourists as the "Plain of Windmills", but few of the thousands of white-sailed windmills exist in working order. That said, the drive to this bowl of rich farmland surrounded by mountains is stunning in itself. Lasithi's patchwork of fertile fields, gardens and orchards strikes a contrast with the treeless grey slopes surrounding it. ◈ *Map M4*

3 Elafonisi

This tiny islet, a stone's throw from the mainland, may in Venetian or Byzantine times have been a preserve for deer, for its name means "deer island". Between Elafonisi and the shore is a lagoon of turquoise water. It is possible to reach the island simply by wading *(see also p46).* ◈ *Map A4*

4 Vai

A group of sturdy date palms on a crescent of sandy beach at Vai is claimed to be Europe's only palm forest. The palms may originally have been planted by Arab raiders or ancient

The White Mountains

Phoenicians. Today the palm grove is carefully protected. ◈ *Map R4*

Omalos Plateau

Lake Votamos (Zaros)
Fed by an underground spring which provides Crete with most of its bottled mineral water, Lake Votamos is a deep blue ring of cool, clear water surrounded by flinty, barren slopes. Tavernas near the shore serve grilled trout from the lake, and a good gorge walk starts nearby. ◈ *Map J5*

Imbros Gorge
The Imbros Gorge extends between the villages of Komitades and Imbros. Its narrowest point is only 2 m (6 ft) wide. It is a three- to four-hour walk. ◈ *Map D4 • 7am–sunset • Adm charge in summer*

Omalos Plateau
A fertile plain, ringed by rocky slopes, lies high up on the northern side of the White Mountains. Millennia of winter rains have washed the topsoil down from the surrounding slopes to create this upland oasis. Most people pass through without stopping, but, especially in spring, this is one of the prettiest, most peaceful spots in Crete. ◈ *Map C3*

Lake Kournas
Terrapins and migrant water birds are among the wildlife to be seen in and around Crete's main body of fresh water. It is prettiest in spring and early summer. ◈ *Map E3*

Kourtaliotiko Gorge
Frogs, terrapins and tiny water snakes splash and slither in freshwater pools at the bottom of the pretty canyon which emerges near Plakias on the south coast. ◈ *Map F4*

Aspros Potamos
The valley of the "white river" – a stream which, like most Cretan watercourses, flows only in winter and spring – opens into the sea at the east end of Makrygialos beach. Surrounded by pines, boulder-covered slopes, terraced fields and olive groves, it makes a pleasant walk. ◈ *Map P5*

Left **Chapel between Agia Roumeli and Loutro** Right **Zakros Gorge**

Mountain Walks

Samaria Gorge

Passing through the ruggedly beautiful scenery of the Samaria National Park, the Samaria Gorge is Crete's most popular walk. The track descends steeply at first from the Omalos plateau, then passes through pine woods, wild flower meadows and ruined, deserted villages to emerge on the Libyan Sea at the small village of Agia Roumeli *(see pp26–27)*.

Samaria Gorge

Across the Lefka Ori

A two-day traverse of the savage, treeless wilderness of the high White Mountains is spectacular, but only for very fit, experienced mountain walkers. The White Mountains rise to summits of almost 2,500 m (8,202 ft), and the climate is bitterly cold in winter and scorchingly hot in summer. ⊗ *Map C–D4*
• *Eos Mountain Refuge, Kallergi • 28210 44647*
• *Open Apr–Oct*

Imbros Gorge

The gorge, which cuts through the western fringes of the White Mountains, is a slightly shorter hike than the better known and much busier Samaria Gorge, but is almost as spectacular and – especially in spring and autumn – allows you to escape from the crowds of day visitors. ⊗ *Map D4*

Sougia-Agia Roumeli

The walk begins in the sleepy beach village of Sougia, on the eastern fringe of the White Mountains, and climbs first through fields and pastureland, then meadows of wild flowers and pine woods, onto barren slopes high above the sea, before descending to Agia Roumeli. Astute navigational skills and a good map are required. ⊗ *Map C4*

Agia Roumeli-Loutro

This one-day walk follows a path along the pebbly beach of Agios Pavlos, then climbs the

Loutro

Lasithi Plateau

steep "Marble Stair" onto a high, pine-wooded plateau, descends into the Aradena Gorge, and finally zig-zags down a steep cliff to the delightful holiday village of Loutro. ⊗ *Map C–D4*

Zakros Gorge

Also known as the "Valley of the Dead", the walk through the Zakros Gorge follows a dry stream bed through eroded limestone cliffs with caves that were used as tombs by the Minoans. ⊗ *Map Q5*

Climbing Mt Idi

The eight-hour ascent of the 2,456-m (8,060-ft) Mt Idi (also called Psiloritis), Crete's highest mountain, begins on the Nida Plateau. An arduous climb, it should be attempted only by experienced walkers. ⊗ *Map H4*

Mt Kofinas

Allow around five hours to climb from the remote village of Kapetaniana to the summit of Kofinas and back. There are fine views of Mt Idi, the Dikti range, and the south coast. ⊗ *Map J6*

Diktian Cave (Lasithi)

The flat, dish-shaped Lasithi Plateau offers easy walking on dirt tracks and paths through fields, olive groves and orchards. Starting from Tzermiadou, the 7-km (4-mile) stroll to the Diktian Cave takes about two hours. ⊗ *Map L5*

E4 European Mountaineering Footpath

Only for very fit and experienced walkers, this is a long, arduous trek with poor route marking, a traverse of the island that takes at least 30 days to complete.
⊗ *Mountaineering Club of Chania, Tzanakaki 90, Chania • 28210 44647*

Mount Idi

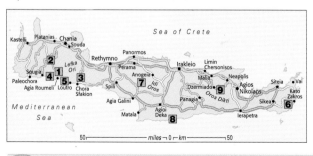

Left **Lammergeier vulture** Right **Scarce swallowtail butterfly**

Wildlife

1 Wild Goat
The Cretan wild goat, or *kri-kri*, is one of Europe's rarest mammals. The shy creature is found in small numbers in the Samaria Gorge National Park, in the heart of the White Mountains and on Dia Island, off Crete's north coast.

Wild goat

Macedonia and Albania, migrates south to the Nile Delta for the winter. A few birds sometimes make landfall in Crete after being blown off course by storms or having become exhausted by the force of strong headwinds.

2 Lammergeier
The rare Lammergeier vulture, Europe's largest bird of prey, may be seen soaring high above the Omalos Plateau or in the high reaches of the White Mountains. Nicknamed the "bone-breaker", the Lammergeier feeds on the carcasses of goats and sheep, and sometimes smashes bones open by dropping them from a great height to get at the marrow.

3 Pelican
The Dalmatian pelican, which breeds in the lakes and wetlands of northern Greece,

4 Eleonora's Falcon
The very rare Eleonora's falcon breeds on some of Crete's offshore islands and can sometimes be seen performing its remarkable aerobatics above the steep cliffs of Zakros, in eastern Crete.

5 Cretan Spiny Mouse
The Cretan spiny mouse is unique to the island. Like most small rodents, it is nocturnal and is therefore not the easiest of the island's mammals to see. Look out for its endearingly large ears and blunt spines against rocky slopes at twilight.

6 Gecko
Big-eyed gecko lizards, with sucker-tipped fingers that enable them to cling to walls and ceilings, inhabit many older buildings, coming out after dark to hunt insects. You may see several clinging to the wall near outdoor

Dalmatian pelicans

Gecko

lamps, waiting to snap up moths and mosquitoes attracted by the light.

Scops Owl
The tiny Scops owl, with its grey plumage and bright yellow eyes, is common in Crete. It nests in holes in battered stone walls and roosts on roadside telephone poles or tree stumps. You are most likely to see Scops owls at dusk, but after dark they can often be heard calling to each other – a monotonous, one-note hoot.

Cretan Argus Butterfly
The beautiful Cretan argus butterfly is limited to the higher slopes of the Dikti and Idi mountains. This large, dark brown butterfly is increasingly endangered through loss of habitat.

Scarce Swallowtail
Europe's largest butterfly is the dramatically patterned scarce swallowtail, its pale yellow wings marked with dark zebra stripes, and red and blue eye-spots. It's a strong flyer and may be seen all over Crete in summer.

Cretan Wild Cat
Cretan shepherds have long claimed that the wilder parts of the island are home to a large wild cat called the *fourokattos*. The first live specimen of this elusive beast was caught in the mid-1990s by Italian zoologists. Weighing 5.5 kg (12 lbs), with a tawny pelt and a formidable snarl, the Cretan wild cat is unique in Europe.

Trees and Flowers

Wild Olive
The wild olive hangs on in the sheltered gorges of Crete's rocky slopes where few other trees thrive.

Cretan Ebony
Putting out spikes of pink flowers in spring, the Cretan ebony clings to steep, rocky cliffs and mountainsides.

Dragon Arum
With its foul-smelling red flower and spike, the dragon arum is a motif in several Minoan frescoes and a reality in shady spots beneath trees.

Yellow Bee Orchid
The yellow bee orchid, bearing flowers that imitate the insects it attracts, blooms profusely on mountain slopes in spring.

Catchfly
The catchfly, with its ragged bright-pink flowers, traps insects on the sap-coated hairs of its sticky stems.

Yellow Horned Poppy
This poppy lends a splash of colour to rocky stretches of the Cretan foreshore.

Giant Reed
The giant calamus reed grows as high as 4 m (13 ft) on the banks of Cretan streams.

Autumn Cyclamen
In October, flowering from apparently barren ground, the autumn cyclamen signals the end of summer.

Spring Crocus
This mauve flower with vivid yellow stamens flowers early in the year.

Evergreen Plane
Endemic to Crete, the tough evergreen plane has evolved to cope with the harsh island environment.

Left **The defeat of Athens by King Minos** Right **Nikos Kazantzakis**

🔟 Famous Cretans

1 Zeus

Paramount among the Greek gods, Zeus was said to have been born and raised in caves *(see p58)*. His mother sheltered him from his child-devouring father, the Titan Kronos, whom Zeus eventually slew, giving rise to a new dynasty of gods.

Zeus

2 King Minos

Minos, King of Crete and both patron and tormentor of the ingenious Daedalos, appears in the Greek myths as a tyrant. In fact, the legendary Minos is probably a composite of many Minoan kings, whose power and wealth were remembered long after their civilization fell.

3 Nicephoros Phokas

The Byzantine general Nicephoros Phokas reconquered Crete from the Saracens in 961. Laying siege to their capital at Khandak (Irakleio), he demoralized the garrison by firing the heads of their captured comrades over the walls of the city.

4 Michael Damaskinos

Michailis Damaskinos (c.1530–91) is the best known of the Cretan School icon

El Greco

painters. Some of his most important works are exhibited in the Museum of Religious Art in Irakleio *(see p13)*.

5 El Greco

Born in the twilight years of Venetian rule in Crete, Domenikos Theotokopoulos (1541–1614) studied the icon painters of the Cretan School; their influence can be seen in the elongated features of his subjects and his vivid use of colour. He trained under Titian in Italy, then moved to Toledo, where he acquired his Spanish nickname of El Greco: "the Greek".

6 Vitsentzos Kornaros

This 16th-century poet (died 1613) was a contemporary of El Greco and Damaskinos and is remembered for his life's work, the *Erotokritos*, post-Byzantine Greece's greatest work of epic literature.

7 Nikos Kazantzakis

Born in Irakleio, Kazantzakis (1883–1957) is best known for his novel *Alexis Zorbas*, translated into English and filmed as *Zorba the Greek*. He was

Discover more at **www.traveldk.com**

Eleftherios Venizelos

excommunicated by the Orthodox Church for his humanist views, and his self-penned epitaph reads: "I hope for nothing. I fear nothing. I am free."

Eleftherios Venizelos

Born at Mournies near Chania, Venizelos (1864–1936) made his reputation in the 1889 and 1896 uprisings. He led the campaign for union with Greece, and went on to become the Greek premier, dominating the nation's politics until the 1930s. He then became involved in a failed republican *coup d'etat* and was forced to flee the country, dying in exile in Paris.

Ioannis Daskalogiannis

Ioannis Daskalogiannis (died 1770) raised the clans of the mountainous and inaccessible Sfakia region in the first major rebellion against Turkey in 1770. The uprising failed, and when Daskalogiannis attempted to negotiate a surrender at Frangokastello he was seized, tortured and skinned alive – a not uncommon penalty for rebels against the sultan.

Chatzimichalis Dalianis

Dalianis garrisoned the fort at Frangokastello with only 385 men during the nationwide uprising in 1828. On the mainland, the rebellion succeeded, giving birth to the modern Greek state, but in Crete it failed. Dalianis and his men, overwhelmingly outnumbered by the Turks, were massacred in a valiant final stand.

Top 10 Works of Art and Literature

1 *Zorba the Greek* by Kazantzakis
The freedom-loving spirit of Greece is to the fore in this early 20th-century tragi-comedy.

2 *Erotokritos* by Vinsentzos Kornaros
Ten thousand lines of epic poetry written in the 15-syllable heptametric style of Byzantium.

3 *Travellers on the Way to the Monastery of St Catherine* by El Greco
El Greco's only painting to be seen in Crete (in the Historical Museum in Knosos).

4 *Lord, Thou Art Great* by Ioannis Kornaros
This is one of Crete's most dazzling and famous icons; it resides at Moni Toplou (see p42).

5 Paintings by Lefteris Kanakakis
Rethymno's Contemporary Arts Centre houses a variety of Kanakakis's work (see p37).

6 *The Bull from the Sea* by Mary Renault
A fictional retelling of the ancient legend of Theseus, Minos and the Minotaur.

7 The Cretan Journal of Edward Lear
Lear's illustrated diary of a journey to Crete in 1864.

8 *Officers and Gentlemen* by Evelyn Waugh
A pithy account of the British in Crete in World War II.

9 *Adoration of the Magi* by Damaskinos
A portrayal of the veneration of the infant Jesus (Museum of Religious Art, Irakleio).

10 Frescoes of Moni Valsamonerou
Variously attributed to Damaskinos and 15th-century painter Konstantinos Rikos.

Left **Hercules and his labours** Right **Theseus and Ariadne in a boat**

TOP 10 Myths and Legends

1 The Birth of Zeus

Zeus was the sixth child of the Titan Kronos, who had devoured his other children to prevent them from overthrowing him as he had overthrown his own father, Uranus, ruler of the old gods. Born in the Diktian Cave in Crete, Zeus was hidden by his mother Rhea and raised in the Idaian Cave on Mount Idi. Zeus eventually poisoned Kronos, making him regurgitate his siblings, who overthrew the Titans to become the new gods and goddesses.

2 Zeus and Europa

Though married to the goddess Hera, Zeus took many mortal lovers, one of whom was the princess Europa, daughter of the King of Phoenicia. Taking the form of a white bull, Zeus carried Europa off to Crete, where he took her as his wife.

Europa on the Bull

3 The Minotaur and the Labyrinth

In the myth of King Minos (one of the sons of Zeus and Europa), his queen Pasiphae bore a child, half bull and half man, after coupling with the sacred bull of Zeus. Minos imprisoned this monster, the Minotaur, in a tortuous maze, the subterranean labyrinth.

The death of Talos

4 Theseus and Ariadne

Minos demanded tribute of youths and maidens from the Athenians after defeating them in war. The victims were given to the Minotaur, but Theseus, prince of Athens, slew the Minotaur and escaped the labyrinth with the help of Minos's daughter Ariadne, who gave him a ball of thread to retrace his steps.

5 Talos the Bronze Giant

According to myth, Zeus created the bronze giant to defend Crete. It patrolled the coasts, hurling huge boulders to sink vessels that came too close. Talos was finally slain by Jason, with the aid of the sorceress Medea, who pointed out the giant's only weak spot, a vein near its ankle.

6 Daedalus and Ikarus

Daedalus and his son, Ikarus, made wings of feathers held together with beeswax in order to escape imprisonment at the hands of King Minos – punishment for helping Theseus slay the Minotaur. Ikarus flew too high and the sun's heat melted the wax, causing him to plummet into the sea, but Daedalus reached safety in Sicily.

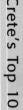

Daedalus and Ikarus

7 Hercules and the Bull of Crete

The demigod Hercules, son of Zeus and the mortal woman Alkmene, was set 12 tasks by King Eurystheus of Argos, one of which was to capture and tame the untameable bull of Crete.

8 Nymphs of Dragolaki

The cave known as the Dragolaki or "Dragon's Lair", just outside the Sfakia mountain village of Agios Ioannis, is said to be haunted by Nereids, water-nymphs who were daughters of the god Nereus.

9 The Immortal Plane Tree at Gortys

Zeus ravished Europa beneath this huge plane tree near the Roman ruins of Gortys. As a result, the tree is said never to shed its leaves, even in winter.

10 The Drossoulites of Frangokastello

Phantoms are said to emerge on 17 May every year from the sea mists and ride into the deserted little fortress at Frangokastello (see p40). They are the ghosts of Chatzimichalis Dalianis (see p57) and his men, massacred by the Turks here in 1828.

Top 10 Caves

1 Sfendoni
Crete's most spectacular cave, crammed with strange rock formations deep beneath the Idi range.

2 Diktian Cave (Diktaion Antron)
Said to be the birthplace of Zeus, this cave above the Lasithi Plateau contains an artificial lake.

3 Idaian Cave
This enormous cavern on the slopes of Mount Idi was Zeus's childhood hideout.

4 Kamares
This cave on Mount Idi's southern face lends its name to the sophisticated Minoan pottery discovered here.

5 Skotino
This is one of Crete's largest caves. It was first dedicated to virgin goddess Britomartis and later became a sanctuary to Artemis.

6 Inatos
The goddess Ilithia, daughter of Zeus and Hera, was worshipped in this grotto, which delves into the sea-cliff above Tsoutsouros.

7 Ilithia
Archaic stone figures of pregnant women have been found in this cave, birthplace of the goddess Ilithia.

8 Profitis Ilias
Like the Diktian Cave, this cave near Arkalochori is also claimed as birthplace of Zeus.

9 Melidoni
This cave was said to be the lair of Talos, the bronze giant created by Zeus.

10 Cave of the Holy Fathers
This gloomy cave in the remote Sellino highlands is now a Greek Orthodox shrine.

Left **Musicians playing the lyra** Centre **Rural piper** Right **Dance performance**

TOP 10 Music and Instruments

Lyra and laouta

1 Lyra
The three-stringed *lyra* is typical of Crete, although the instrument is also found in mainland Greece. It is similar in shape to a violin, but has a far more rounded, pear-shaped body and the neck is stouter. The *lyra* player props the instrument on one knee and plays it with a small bow, producing melodies and harmonies that may be merry, martial or melancholy.

2 Laouta
The *laouta* is the Cretan version of the mandolin and is one of the most important instruments for Cretan musicians and composers. It is usually used to provide a backing rhythm for the *lyra,* and like the *lyra* is an essential member of any Cretan ensemble. However, the *laouta* is sometimes also heard as a solo instrument.

3 Bouzouki
The eight-stringed *bouzouki* is an eastern relative of the guitar and its origins are probably in Asia Minor. *Bouzouki* music gained popularity in mainland Greece after the exchange of Greek and Turkish populations in the 1920s, but the *bouzouki* has always been in use in Crete.

4 Santouri
The hammer dulcimer or *santouri* is another import from Asia Minor into Greece, where it was not widely played until the 1920s, though Alexis Zorbas, hero of *Zorba the Greek*, claimed playing the *santouri* among his many talents.

5 Gerakokoudouna (Hawk Bells)
Cretan *lyra* players sometimes attach tiny copper or silver hawk bells to the horsehair bows with which the *lyra* is played. These little bells, as well as having an ornamental purpose, can be made to provide an occasional lively and rhythmic jingling accompaniment.

Musicians outside a local kafeneia, traditional café

Discover more at **www.traveldk.com**

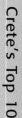

The askomandoura

Diouli
The *diouli* is a small hand drum of wood and goatskin which in a traditional Greek music ensemble represents the entire percussion section.

Voulgari
The *voulgari*, a Cretan version of the long-necked lute known in Turkey as the *saz*, was a popular solo instrument in Cretan village music but is rarely heard now.

Askomandoura (Bagpipe)
The *askomandoura*, or Greek bagpipe, was once a popular instrument around the southern Aegean islands. Like some other seldom heard instruments, it is undergoing a minor revival as a new wave of younger musicians rediscover their musical roots.

Kithara (Guitar)
The guitar, whether acoustic or (more often) electric, has sadly ousted many of the older instruments and, even at village festivals, weddings and saints days, has become a standard member of the Cretan ensemble.

Baglamas
Not unique to Crete, this stringed instrument was the poor man's makeshift *bouzouki*, home-made with a dried gourd or sometimes a tortoiseshell for a sound box and wire strings.

Top 10 Traditional Songs and Dances

Haniotis
The *haniotis* is a dignified line dance for men and women that comes from Chania.

Pidiktos
The *pidiktos*, a dance from eastern Crete, involves great athletic leaps and bounds.

Pentozalis
The *pentozalis's* sprightly rhythms are reminiscent of the jigs and reels of Irish and Scottish folk music.

Sousta
A flirtatious dance for the young, and a favourite at weddings and festivals.

Hasapikos ("Zorba's Dance")
The *hasapikos* or "butcher's dance" provided inspiration for "Zorba's Dance" in the film *Zorba the Greek*.

Siganos
The dignified *siganos* for groups of men and woman is a dance for any festival.

Mandinades
The traditional rhyming couplets – usually love songs – are typical of Crete's rich oral tradition, which comes to the fore in local festivals.

Rizitiko
The *rizitiko* is Crete's warrior dance, in which male performers act out scenes of combat and heroism.

Syrtos
Performed all over Greece, the *syrtos* is the best known of the Greek circle dances.

Rembetika
The Greek version of the urban blues, brought to Greece by refugees from Asia Minor in the 1920s, is popular with young Cretans.

Left **Traditional Greek dancing** Right **Lighting candles for the Virgin Mary**

Festivals and Events

An Easter meal with bread and dyed eggs

Easter

This is the most important celebration of the Greek year. It is predominantly a family affair, focusing on the home, where spit-roasted goat is the highlight of a day of eating and drinking. More formal, religious processions are led by fabulously attired priests or monks and are often followed by fireworks. In many towns and villages, Easter culminates with the burning of an effigy of Judas Iscariot.

Moni Arkadiou

Festival of the Virgin Mary, 15 Aug

The Festival of the Virgin Mary *(Apokimisis tis Panayias)* is second only to Easter and tends to be a much more public celebration. Church processions are followed by open-air eating and drinking in the churchyard or village square, in turn followed by music and dancing until the early hours.

Arkadiou, 7–9 Nov

A patriotic three-day gathering to commemorate the freedom fighters of the 1866 uprising and the defenders of Moni Arkadiou, who blew themselves up rather than surrender to the Turks.

Sultanina, Siteia, first two weeks Aug

Siteia's sultana festival is a relaxed celebration of the grape harvest, with music, dancing, lashings of local wine and nightly performances in the old Venetian fortress, now restored as an open air theatre.

Chestnut Festival, mid-Oct

This festival of the chestnut harvest is most fervently celebrated in the village of Elos in southwest Crete. Music, dancing, eating and drinking all play their part.

Festival of St Nicholas, Agios Nikolaos, 6 Dec

Many processions and celebrations abound at Agios Nikolaos to celebrate the town's patron saint, who is also venerated all over the island.

Roasting goat on the spit at Easter

7 Epiphany, 6 Jan

In the Greek calendar, Epiphany ends the 12-day reign of mischievous spirits who run loose during

Diving at Epiphany

Christmas. Ceremonial rites banish the spirits until the next year, and baptismal fonts, springs and wells are blessed by local priests or monks. In some places such as Chora Sfakion, young men dive for a crucifix tossed into the harbour by a priest.

8 Independence Day/Feast of the Annunciation, 25 Mar

A national festival commemorating the beginning of Greece's final struggle for independence in 1821. It is combined with the celebration of the Feast of the Annunciation, and so religious processions are followed by military parades in major towns, along with music and dancing all the way.

9 St George's Day, 23 Apr

At the Church of Asi Gonia Apokoronou near Rethymno, hundreds of Cretan shepherds bring their sheep to be blessed on St George's Day each year, hoping to ensure healthy flocks and a prosperous year. In return, the shepherds distribute free sheep's milk.

10 Festival of Agios Titos, 25 Aug

The biggest celebration to mark the day of Crete's patron saint is at Irakleio, where icons and relics are carried through the streets with great pomp. The saint's day is also celebrated at churches across the island.

Top 10 Saints

1 Agios Titos (St Titus)
This follower of St Paul was given the task of bringing Christianity to the Cretans.

2 Agios Nikolaos (St Nicholas)
The patron saint of seafarers and fishermen is honoured all around the coast of Crete.

3 Agios Pavlos (St Paul)
The chapel of Agios Pavlos stands where the saint was swept ashore between Agia Roumeli and Loutro.

4 Agios Michalis (St Michael)
The commander of the heavenly host is especially revered by combative Cretans.

5 Agios Georgios (St George)
The patron saint of shepherds is greatly esteemed and, as a warrior saint, is doubly popular.

6 Agios Eftihios (St Eustacius)
St Eustacius is especially popular in southwest Crete, where many chapels and children bear his name.

7 Ag. Ioannis Theologos (St John the Divine)
St John wrote the *Book of Revelations* on Patmos, but he is also venerated on Crete.

8 Profitis Ilias (Prophet Elijah)
Many mountain-top chapels for this prophet may originally have been for the sun-god Helios.

9 Agioi Deka (Ten Saints)
Ten Cretan martyrs killed for their faith by the Romans have their church near Gortys.

10 Ag. Ioannis Prodromos (St John the Baptist)
St John is often shown in Greek art wearing goat-skin breeches, like the pre-Christian god Pan.

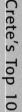

Crete's Top 10

Left **Odos Souliou, Rethymno** Centre **Odos Daedalou, Irakleio** Right **Honey at a market stall**

Markets and Shopping Streets

1 Chania Market, Plateia Venizelou, Chania

Odos Skridlof, Chania

The market building is a Chania landmark and bustles with vendors and shoppers. A visual feast and also the place to buy herbs, olive oil, dried fruit, honey and typical Cretan souvenirs, such as the tiny metal pots used to brew Greek coffee. ✎ *Map D2/B6*

2 Odos Skridlof, Chania
Running through the centre of the old quarter, this has been a street of saddlemakers and cobblers for centuries, perhaps even millennia. These days, satchels, sandals and handbags abound. ✎ *Map D2/B6*

3 Boutari Winery, Archanes
The best wines in Crete (and from other parts of Greece) can be tasted and bought in this visitor centre at Crete's top winery on the Fantaxommetocho vineyard *(see also p81)*. ✎ *70100 Archanes • 28107 31617 • Map K4*

4 Odos 1866, Irakleio
Irakleio's main market street and a great place to shop for Cretan herbs and tisanes. It also offers an insight into the Cretan diet – along with the olives, you will see buckets of live snails for sale. ✎ *Map K3*

5 Odos Daedalou, Irakleio
Named after the legendary inventor of the Labyrinth *(see p58)*, this road is rather more upmarket than Odos 1866, and is lined with shops selling jewellery and linen and cotton clothes to summer visitors. ✎ *Map K3*

6 Museum Shops
For quality replicas of finds from the archaeological sites of Crete, visit the Museum Shops, in the former Venetian Loggia on Odos Paleologou in Rethymno and in the Byzantine Museum in Chania. ✎ *Map Q2/A5*

7 Local Products Exhibition, Farmers' Union of Siteia
Promoting the produce of local farmers, this co-operative venture is well worth visiting just to see how the vines and olives of Crete are grown and processed. It is also a good place for quality olive oil, wine and *raki*, Crete's favourite spirit. ✎ *Myssonos 74 • Map Q4 • Open by appt: call 28430 29991*

Souvenir shop, Irakleio

8 Odos Souliou, Rethymno

Rethymno's upmarket shopping street, lined with stores selling copies of Minoan pottery, traditional Cretan pottery and modern ceramics, as well as colourful cotton and linen, lace and embroidery. ◈ *Map F3/Q2*

9 Odos Ethnikis Andistasi, Rethymno

The most photogenic market in Crete spills out – as indeed it has for centuries – from open-fronted shops and stalls along Odos Ethnikis Andistasi and around the Venetian Porta Guora. Go early in the morning, when it is in full cry and waiters bustle from stall to stall with coffee and *raki*. ◈ *Map F3/Q2*

10 Car Park next to Municipal Gardens, Rethymno

An open-air market takes place every Thursday from 7am until 1pm. Stalls sell local produce, fruit and vegetables, cheese, honey, flowers and clothing. There is also a smaller market on Saturday mornings in the square next to the bus station. ◈ *Map F3*

Top 10 Traditional Shops

1 Xilouris Popular Art, Anogeia
The ancient art of handloom weaving. ◈ *Milopotamou*

2 Cretan Handicraft, Mirthios
Vividly coloured weavings, shepherds' sticks, embroidery, lace, herbs, wines, *raki* and olive oil. ◈ *74060 Mirthios*

3 To Maxairadiko, Chania
The best of a clutch of traditional knifemakers on the street. ◈ *18 Sifakas*

4 Voskakis Workshop, Amari Valley
Nikos Voskakis hand-carves olive wood platters, bowls, dishes, candlesticks and cutlery. ◈ *Bizari*

5 Nikos Siragas, Rethymno
Artistic wood-turner acquiring an international reputation for his beautiful handmade bowls, vases and works of art. ◈ *Petalioti 2, Rethymno*

6 Landen Apan, Chania
Traditional foodstuffs of Crete. ◈ *Daskalogianni 70*

7 Ypsanta Selinou, Paleochora
Tiny shop on a nameless lane, with tapestries, rugs and lace. ◈ *Off main street*

8 Top Hanas, Chania
Wonderful stock of old Cretan rugs, blankets and kilims. ◈ *3 Angelou*

9 Roka Carpets, Chania
Cretan textile weaving. ◈ *Zambeliou 61*

10 Komboloi 52, Chania
Old-fashioned rosaries made from olive wood, amber, jet, turquoise etc. ◈ *Dimotiki Agora 52*

Porta Guora, Rethymno

Left **Dining in a traditional taverna** Centre **Greek coffee** Right **Octopuses hanging out to dry**

🔟 Food and Drink

1 Tsikoudia

Tsikoudia or *raki* (like Italian grappa) is a colourless spirit distilled from the skins and stems left after grape pressing. You may see market traders starting the day with a shot of *tsikoudia* and a strong coffee. It is also drunk after meals.

Tsikoudia, strong spirit

2 Retsina

Retsina is a white wine flavoured with pine resin. The flavour was originally imparted by the pine storage barrels, but today the resin is added before bottling. It is often served chilled, though locally made *retsina* may be available from the barrel *(apo to bareli)*, traditionally being served in copper jugs.

3 Wines

Cretan wines are becoming more sophisticated as makers introduce techniques pioneered by New World producers. The Boutari company's Fantaxo-metocho vineyard at Archanes *(see p81)*, where award-winning white wines are made, offers a guided tour, tasting opportunities and a shop.

4 Olives

Olives and Greece are inseparable. Indeed, without the olive – which has provided not only food but also oil for lamps, wood for fuel and timber for building ships and homes – Crete might not have become the cradle of Minoan civilization. Olives are sold in a bewildering array of sizes and flavours, with as many as 40 different types available from all over Greece.

5 Cheeses (Staka and Mizithra)

Far more delicious than the ubiquitous feta are Crete's own cheeses, such as *mizithra*, made from fresh sheep's milk, and *staka*, made from whey.

6 Cretan Sausages (Loukanika)

Loukanika – small spicy pork sausages – are found all over Greece, but those from Crete are reckoned to be among the best. They may be served fried (*tiganita*) or smoked (*kapnista*), and are a regular feature of a lavish meze (dish of appetizers).

Left **Green and black olives** Right **Cretan cheeses**

Loukanika, the spicy Cretan sausages

Herbs

1 Dittany
Taking its name from the Dikti mountains, this variety of oregano is unique to Crete and has long been credited with restorative powers.

2 Sage
Sage from the Cretan mountains is a favourite medicinal *tisane*, and is said to cure fever, chills, sore throats and rheumatism.

3 Saffron
Deriving from the crocus flower, costly saffron is used sparingly to add colour and flavour to soups and stews.

4 Thyme
Sweet-scented thyme, with its deep purple flowers, grows wild on Crete's roadsides and hillsides.

5 Coriander
Coriander is used fresh as a flavouring and garnish for stews, grills and salads.

6 Cinnamon
Cretans acquired a taste for spices during the Turkish and Venetian trading eras. Today, cinnamon flavours desserts like *rizokalo* (rice pudding) and sweet pies.

7 Cumin
Another exotic import, cumin is essential in the slowly cooked casserole *stifado*.

8 Rosemary
Growing in abundance, rosemary is used by Cretans mainly to flavour fish dishes.

9 Mint
This ubiquitous wild herb scents the air on rural walks and flavours dozens of dishes.

10 Fennel
Growing profusely in the countryside, this member of the aniseed family is used to flavour ouzo, the national drink.

7 Greek Coffee (Kafe Elliniko)
Finely ground coffee and sugar are boiled together in small metal pots to make a thick, black drink, which is served in a tiny cup along with a tall glass of water. To order a sweet coffee, ask for *glykou*; for medium-sweet, ask for *metriou*; and for coffee without sugar order *skieto*.

8 Snails (Saligkaria)
Once a valuable source of protein in hard times, snails are now regarded as a delicacy. *Saligkaria stifado* (snail casserole) is a uniquely Cretan dish, and is unlikely to be found on the menu in tourist restaurants.

9 Soup (Kreatosoupa and Patsa)
Cretan peasant cooking makes full use of any animal slaughtered. *Kreatosoupa* (meat soup) is made from the bones and left-over scraps of goat, mutton or beef, while *patsa* is a rich soup made with tripe. Both are often served at festivals, when a goat is traditionally slaughtered and spit-roasted as a family meal.

10 Octopus
Octopus *(oktapodi)* are caught by spear fishing, tenderized by pounding on a rock, then hung to dry in the sun before being grilled over charcoal or cooked in a casserole *(stifado)* with onions and cumin.

Left **Portes, Chania** Centre **The Old Mill, Elounda** Right **Veneto, Rethymno**

Restaurants

Tamam, Chania
Popular with Chania's locals as well as holidaymakers, Tamam has a menu that takes in cuisine from right around the shores of the Eastern Mediterranean. Good choice for vegetarians too *(see p101)*.

Portes, Chania
Presenting traditional Greek favourites with a modern twist, Portes stands out for its original cooking. Try the daily specials prepared with local ingredients *(see p101)*.

Amphissa olives

The Old Mill, Elounda
The most luxurious dining on the Elounda Peninsula is in the gourmet restaurant of the Elounda Mare hotel *(see p126)*. The menu is fabulous, combining the best of Greek cooking with world-class

Courtyard at Avli, Rethymno

cuisine, and dining is accompanied by piano music. There are only 20 covers, so booking well ahead is essential. The dress code is formal *(see p113)*.

Plateia, Mirthios
This village taverna draws crowds for the views from its terrace over the coast towards Africa. Half of Crete seems to turn up on Sundays, but it is quieter during the week, with more time to enjoy the traditional cuisine and the laid-back ambience *(see p101)*.

Avli, Rethymno
This elegant courtyard restaurant is, arguably, the best in Rethymno. A pretty garden provides the setting for the traditional grilled and roasted meat dishes, served alongside traditional Cretan favourites such as *apatzia* (smoked sausages) and roast goat *(see p101)*.

Veneto, Rethymno
The 13th-century vaults that house the Veneto once contained a refectory for monks living in the cells above. The Veneto's menu features a number of Cretan specialities, and service is excellent *(see p101)*.

Loukoulos, Irakleio
More formal than the average Cretan restaurant, Loukoulos is a haven in the heart of busy Irakleio. Choose between eating

Discover more at **www.traveldk.com**

Loukoulos, Irakleio

in the garden courtyard or the elegantly decorated dining rooms. The food is Italian with a distinct Greek influence, as well as the odd touch of French gastronomy *(see p89)*.

Poulis, Elounda
In a beautiful location on the waterfront, Poulis even has tables on a floating pontoon; lit up at night, it feels like you are dining on a yacht. The fish, octopus and calamari are excellent and the traditional meze are exceptional *(see p113)*.

Pelagos, Agios Nikolaos
An elegant mansion and its leafy garden courtyard make an appropriately stylish setting for the delicious Cretan food served at Pelagos, probably the best in Agios Nikolaos *(see p113)*.

Balcony, Siteia
Run by a Cretan-French couple in a renovated Neo-Classical building, Balcony offers Greek fusion cooking with Mexican, Asian and French influences. Wild herbs and local produce are extensively used in dishes ranging from traditional Cretan snails with tomato and goat's cheese to pork fillet with yogurt and pilaf rice *(see p113)*.

Top 10 Fish Served in Cretan Restaurants

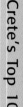

1 Fagri
Red sea bream, prized for its delicate white flesh, is grilled and served whole and is one of the most expensive fish dishes on the menu.

2 Melanourgia
A large, silver-scaled fish with tasty white flesh; it's usually grilled.

3 Barbounia
Small red mullet appear on almost every tourist menu, pan-fried or grilled. Each fish provides only a few delicious mouthfuls – beware of bones!

4 Marides
Tiny whitebait are dipped in flour and shallow-fried, then served with shredded lettuce and a slice of lemon.

5 Lavraki
Sea bass is baked in olive oil, red wine vinegar and rosemary, served whole.

6 Sardelles
Sardines are often wrapped in vine leaves to seal in flavour and moisture, then grilled. Salted and pickled sardines are often served as meze.

7 Xifias
Swordfish keeps its flavour well when frozen, so is a favourite with restaurateurs.

8 Skorpios
The evil-looking scorpion fish is surprisingly tasty and essential in fish soup.

9 Tonnos
Tuna steaks are best savoured in spring and autumn, when tuna migrate through Cretan waters.

10 Gopes
Nondescript-looking, bony little fish that's the cheapest on the menu, but delicious once the bones are removed.

For more restaurants around Crete See p89, p101 & p113

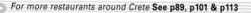

Left **Fresh fish** Centre **Ta Douliana, Douliana** Right **Vegetables ripening in the sun**

🔟 Rural Tavernas

1 Sterna tou Bloumosifi, Vamos

This taverna is a key part of a restored 19th-century stone village. It serves a wide menu of Cretan specialities, baked in wood-burning ovens, and is open for breakfast, lunch and dinner *(see p101)*.

Taverna habitués

2 Ta Douliana, Douliana

Situated in the centre of tiny Douliana, this typical village taverna's rickety wooden tables and chairs are on a pretty terrace shaded by vines. The menu focuses on traditional, hearty fare such as *arni avgolemono* (lamb with lemon sauce). There is also a good selection of local cheeses and wines. ◎ *Centre of Douliana, on road between Kalive and Vamos • Map E3 • 28250 23380 • Closed Mon • €€*

3 Taverna Goules, Goulediana

This traditional village taverna offers Cretan food with a twist. A highlight of the menu is the roast pork in wine and honey sauce. ◎ *10 km (6 miles) south of Rethymno • Map F4 • 28310 41001 • €€*

4 Aetos, Anogeia

A meat-eater's paradise, this taverna offers delicious slow-roasted lamb – butterflied and cooked over charcoal in an outdoor oven. Aetos also makes the most of other local produce, with some fine mountain cheeses and plenty of home-grown salads and vegetables *(see p89)*.

5 Taverna tou Zisi, Rethymno

Zisi looks rather unprepossessing at first, housed in a drab concrete building. But inside, it serves some of the best food around – the charcoal-grilled lamb alone is worth a trip from Rethymno *(see p101)*.

6 Kalliotzina, Koutsouras

A classic island taverna, Kalliotzina serves traditional Cretan cuisine cooked in extra virgin

Sterna tou Bloumosifi, Vamos

For price bands **See p89**

Kalliotzina, Koutsouras

olive oil. There is no written menu, so visit the kitchen to check out what's on offer. It has live Greek music twice a week *(see p113)*.

El Greco, Lendas
In traditional taverna fashion, El Greco has the day's baked dishes displayed in the kitchen for you to choose from. Other dishes include locally caught fish, octopus and grilled meats, served on a series of terraces above the beach. Book in advance *(see p89)*.

Taverna Androulidakis, Gonia
Come to this family-run taverna for atmospheric alfresco summer dining. The extensive menu of Cretan favourites features dishes prepared with home-grown produce. ✆ *Map F3 • 28310 31282 • €€*

Erotokritos, Ammoudara
Popular with locals and tourists alike, Erotokritos is big, with an impressive stone dining room. It offers an extensive menu with a huge selection of delicious Greek starters *(see p89)*.

Piperia, Pefki
Piperia serves Cretan dishes prepared from locally sourced ingredients. Visitors can enjoy delicious food along with spectacular views of the coast and a laid-back ambience. At night, there may be live music and dancing. ✆ *Map P5 • 28430 52471 • €€*

Top 10 Cretan Wines

1 Domaine Fantaxometocho
Excellent red wine made from Mantilaria and Kotsifali grapes. Good with lamb or chicken.

2 Chardonnay Boutari
Dry, white varietal wine – great with seafood and cheese.

3 Sauvignon Blanc Boutari
Dry white, ideal with vegetable dishes, cheeses and cold cuts.

4 Sant'Antonio
Produced from Kotsifali and Mantilaria grapes in the Peza region of central Crete by Miliarakis Brothers, this deep red wine is barrel-aged for five to six years.

5 Kokolakis
Ioannis Kokolakis bottles wines made from liatiko grapes grown in the Agrilos vineyards, not far from Siteia, which produce a light, dry red wine.

6 Kissamos
This potent red wine with a 13 per cent alcohol content comes from Romeiko grapes grown in Crete's north west.

7 Rodolino
Made from liatiko red wine grapes blended with white varieties, this rosé is best served chilled to the bone.

8 Clos de Creta
Unassuming white wine made from Romeiko grapes from the Kissamos area.

9 Domenico
Made from Vilana and Rozaki grapes, this is one of the better pine-flavoured *retsinas*.

10 Malvasia
One of Europe's oldest wines, Malvasia was exported as far as England by the Venetians. Made from a blend of sugar-rich, aromatic grapes, it is best drunk with dessert.

Left **Fortetza, Chania** Right **Kali Kardia, Siteia**

Cafés and Ouzeries

View of cafés lining Rethymno harbour

1 Pagopoieion, Irakleio
Housed in a former ice factory, the decor of this stunning, fashionable café-bar preserves many original features. A wide range of wines and coffees is served. There's often live jazz or other events (see p88).

2 Ouzeri Terzaki, Irakleio
A favourite among locals, Terzaki is one of a row of ouzeris lining the narrow alley heading down to the harbour. There are substantial meals on the menu; however, a drink and a selection of meze (such as their cheese-stuffed artichoke) is particularly recommended. ◈ Marineli 17 • Map T1 • 28102 21444

3 Kirkor, Irakleio
A classic café right by the Morosini fountain, Kirkor has tables spreading out into the square. The speciality is bougatsa, a creamy cheese pie sprinkled with sugar and cinnamon. With a variety of coffees and an array of diet-busting delicacies, it makes a perfect spot for breakfast (see p88).

4 Fortetza, Chania
Delightful café-bar midway along the mole that encloses the Venetian harbour. This is the best place in town for a sunset drink, with views across the water to the old town. ◈ Palaio Limani • Map D2/B4

5 Kaaren's, Elounda
Check out this café's delicious breakfast, brunch, lunch and early evening cocktails for a welcome change from the regular taverna fare (see p112).

6 Apicorno Café, Kalives
An attractive modern café with large indoor and outdoor seating areas. Open all day until late throughout the year, it serves a variety of coffee, ice cream and alcoholic drinks as well as a choice of breakfasts and snacks. ◈ Main Street • Map E2

Pagopoieion café-bar, Irakleio

Typical rural Cretan café

Avli, Agios Nikolaos

This delightful garden ouzeri is set in a courtyard shaded by grapevines and lemon trees. Excellent meze as well as more elaborate dishes are served with a good white wine made from the owner's own grapes.
⊗ P Georgiou 12 • Map N4
• 28410 82479

Mesostrati, Rethymno

A range of Cretan specialities and drinks is served at this traditional Cretan café/meze bar. Enjoy a coffee or *raki* on the shady terrace while watching the hustle and bustle of the town.
⊗ Kounoupa Lelas • Map F3

Kafenio Rakadiko, Siteia

Located right on the waterfront, this very traditional *kafeneion* allows patrons to enjoy a great view with their Greek coffee *(see p112)*.

Kali Kardia, Siteia

Frequented more by locals than visitors, Kali Kardia ("Good Heart") makes few concessions to tourist tastes. Authentic meze, from local cheeses to grilled snails, are washed down with strong Cretan *retsina* straight from the barrel.
⊗ Foundalidou 28 • Map Q4

Meze Dishes

1 Octopus (Oktapodi)
A favourite accompaniment to a glass of *ouzo*, *raki* or *retsina* is a dish of octopus chunks, cooked in oil, herbs and vinegar, and served cold.

2 Marides
Tiny whitebait are coated in flour, flash-fried and served with a slice of lemon as a snack or a first course.

3 Loukanika
These smoked and spiced pork sausages are a typically Cretan snack, served often in winter.

4 Baked Potatoes
Another typical winter snack served in mountain village ouzeries, often cooked in a wood-burning stove in the middle of the café.

5 Saganaki
A salty and aromatic cheese-based appetizer served fried or grilled as a meze dish.

6 Karpousi
Sweet and refreshing pink cubes of chilled watermelon are among the most popular summertime meze.

7 Olives
You will see more than 40 different kinds of olive for sale in Greek markets. Their strong flavours complement a glass of *retsina* wonderfully.

8 Gigantes
A more substantial dish: large white beans simmered in oil, herbs and tomatoes. Served cold in summer.

9 Spanakopites
Tiny spinach pies made with flaky filo pastry.

10 Melitzanosalata
A delicious savoury dip made by pureeing grilled aubergines with herbs, usually served with crusty bread.

For more places to eat and drink in Crete
See pp68–9, 70–71, 88–9, 100–101, 112–113

Left **Buzzing bars, Chersonisos** Right **Tavernas, Agia Galini**

Nightlife

1 Chersonisos
If you're a summer party animal, Chersonisos is the place for you. Not far from the airport, this former fishing village has become a continuous strip of bars, clubs, restaurants and guesthouses stretching along one of Crete's best beaches. A multinational (but mainly British) clientele (see also p86). ⊗ Map L3

New York Bar, Hersonisos

2 Malia
Malia rivals its neighbour Chersonisos as a nightlife hot spot. It has been a party town for some 30 years, and its main street is lined with cocktail bars, restaurants, video bars and dance clubs. Along this stretch, happy hour can last most of the evening (see also p86). ⊗ Map M4

3 Platanias
Platanias is where most of Chania's younger residents go to party on summer weekends.

There are at least a dozen great clubs, most with open-air dance floors, and things do not really start to get lively until well after midnight (see also p98). ⊗ Map C2

4 Paleochora
A hippy hideout well into the 1980s (see p92), Paleochora's nightlife is still laid-back to a fault. A handful of relaxed – and none too noisy – music bars are scattered along the Pebble Beach waterfront, where, just out of town, there are a couple of open-air discos. ⊗ Map B4

5 Agios Nikolaos
Agios Nikolaos has a surprisingly lively after-dark scene, compared with its day-time placidity. The town's nightlife hot spot is Odos 25 Martiou (running uphill from the southeast corner of the harbour), where there are half a dozen or more music bars, with as many again around the harbour. The town's dance club scene is more limited, with only one or two full-on clubs (see also p103). ⊗ Map N4

6 Rethymno
Most of the liveliest music-bars are in the streets inland

Café Zargos, Agios Nikolaos

from the harbour. Later on, the nightlife scene shifts to the open-air discos and clubs in the resort area, along the seafront east of the centre *(see also pp22–3)*. ◈ Map F3

Nightlife on Venizelou, central Siteia

Irakleio

Not many holidaymakers stay in Crete's capital *(see pp12–13)*, so its nightlife scene is more staid than in the resorts. Young locals congregate in the cafés and music bars around Plateia Venizelou and Odos Chandakou, but the discos near the harbour are rather seedy. ◈ Map K3

Chania

Music blasts out from most of the cafés and bars along the harbour front at Chania in the summer, and if you prefer an evening of bar-hopping and café-crawling to a night in the dance

Chania's harbour front at night

clubs, there are few better places in the whole of Crete. Most younger Chaniots, however, desert the cafés for the clubs of Platanias after the toll of midnight *(see also pp18–19)*. ◈ Map D2

Agia Galini

A small resort *(see p86)* that has made catering to the party crowd its specialism. Things get lively by 11pm in a cluster of bars and dance clubs around the harbour, where you can club-hop until the early hours. ◈ Map G5

Siteia

The nightlife is a good deal less frenzied here than at other resorts along the north coast, but many a pleasant evening can be spent wandering from bar to bar along the waterfront. There are half a dozen good dance clubs *(see also p103)*. ◈ Map Q4

AROUND THE ISLAND

CRETE'S TOP 10

Left **Malia at sunrise** Centre **Café, Irakleio market** Right **Agia Galini harbour**

Central Crete

THE LANDSCAPES OF CENTRAL CRETE *include some of the island's best beaches, rolling farmland where vines and olives flourish, and rugged mountains – among them, Crete's highest summit, Mt Idi, or Psiloritis. This was the heartland of Minoan civilization, and the most important Minoan ruins lie just south of the island's modern capital, Irakleio. Along the north coast are some busy holiday resorts, while on the south coast, there are quieter, smaller places to enjoy a beach holiday in the sun.*

Traditional Cretan gateway, Chersonisos

🔟 Sights in Central Crete

1. Ancient Knosos
2. Phaestos
3. Gortys
4. Irakleio
5. Diktian Cave
6. Lasithi
7. Mt Idi
8. Kaszantzakis Museum
9. Agia Triada
10. Boutari Winery and Audio-Visual Show

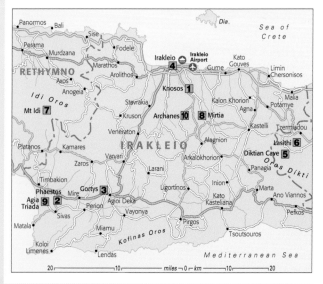

Previous pages **Preveli beach**

South propylon, Knosos

Ancient Knosos
Knosos was pinpointed as an important archaeological site by the great Heinrich Schliemann and unearthed by British archaeologist Arthur Evans less than 100 years ago. The columns, courtyards and coloured frescoes of this ancient Minoan palace still have the power to amaze. Knosos was lost to history after the cataclysmic volcanic eruption that destroyed the Minoan civilization, but the site is now one of the most impressive relics of the vanished world of the Minoans (see pp8–11).

Phaestos
This labyrinth of ruins dating from around 1600 BC includes a Minoan courtyard and theatre with tiers of stone seats, a monumental stairway, peristyle

Phaestos

hall and a vast central courtyard. The still undeciphered Phaestos Disc, which was discovered here, is on display in the Irakleio Archaeological Museum (see p14). Phaestos was destroyed around 1450 BC by the cataclysm that also laid low the rest of Crete's Minoan palaces. Not usually as crowded as the more famous Knosos, the site at Phaestos has an impressive location on a hillside above fertile farmland (see pp20–21).

The praetorium, Gortys

Gortys
Toppled Roman columns, a ruined Byzantine basilica, post-Minoan fortifications, and an agora, acropolis and remains of temples to Athena and Apollo all hint at the past glories of this large and little-visited archaeological site close to Crete's south coast. First settled in Minoan times, it became one of the most important cities of Doric Crete. It later allied itself with the Romans to become an important provincial capital, and was one of Crete's most prosperous cities until it was sacked by Arab invaders during the anarchic years of the 8th century AD (see pp24–5).

Irakleio harbour

4 Irakleio

The modern capital of Crete was badly damaged in World War II, and few of its old Venetian buildings survived the reconstruction of the city. However, its Venetian fortress, harbour, arsenal and city walls are still impressive. For a morning's itinerary, see pages 82–3. The city's main attraction is the Irakleio Archaeological Museum *(see pp14–15)*.

5 Diktian Cave

According to ancient Greek myths, this mossy cavern, filled with strange limestone formations, was the birthplace of the greatest Olympian god, Zeus. Rhea, Zeus's mother, supposedly hid the young godling from his father, Kronos, here. Bronze figurines and Minoan double axes found in the cave are on show in the Irakleio Archaeological Museum. The site is also often referred to as the Psychro Cave. *Map L5*

6 Lasithi

The so-called "Plain of Windmills" is a high plain of fertile farmland surrounded by bare grey limestone hills. Its nickname is misleading, though. Only a few rusting metal derricks remain of the famed

Ruin, Lasithi

The Knosos Enigma?

Most archaeologists accept Sir Arthur Evans' view that the enigmatic maze of ruins at Knosos was a royal palace, the bustling hub of the greatest empire that the islands of the Aegean had ever seen. But a few "heretical" archaeologists now claim that Knosos may actually have been a giant necropolis where kings and nobles were interred, as in the tombs of ancient Egypt. The debate continues.

white-sailed windmills that once dotted the plateau in their hundreds. However, Lasithi is still worth a visit for the spectacular drive through the mountains and the glimpses it offers of a traditional way of life. *Map M4*

7 Mt Idi

At 2,456 m (8,060 ft), Mt Idi, which is also known as Mt Ida and Mt Psiloritis, is Crete's highest mountain. Only fit, experienced and well-equipped mountain walkers should try the eight-hour hike to its summit and back. However, it is possible to drive as far as the Nida Plateau, 1,400 m (4,600 ft) above sea level, from which there are spectacular views. *Map G–H4*

8 Kazantzakis Museum

Cretan author Nikos Kazantzakis (1883–1957) is best known outside Greece for the novel *Alexis Zorbas*, which is set in Crete during the early 20th century. The book was filmed in 1964 as *Zorba the Greek*, starring Anthony Quinn in the title role. Kazantzakis' outspoken humanism led the Orthodox church to regard him as a heretic. The author was born in Mirtia, and a small museum in the Kazantzakis family home is crammed with his manuscripts and diaries, photos and other memorabilia. ⊗ *Map K4 • Mirtia village square, signposted • 28107 41689 • Mar–Oct: 9am–5pm Wed–Sun; Nov–Feb: 10am–3pm Sun • Adm • www.kazantzakis-museum.gr*

9 Agia Triada

Excavated by Italian archaeologists at the beginning of the 20th century, Agia Triada is smaller than other Minoan sites such as Knosos and Phaestos and was probably an aristocratic villa or a royal summer palace. Some of the finest Minoan pottery, including three carved stone vases, was discovered here and is displayed in the Irakleio Archaeological Museum. Agia Triada is only 3 km (2 miles) west of Phaestos, so can easily be visited on the same day.

Agia Triada

Because Agia Triada draws fewer visitors than the larger sites, you can explore its honeycomb of stone corridors, stairs and courtyards at your own pace. ⊗ *Map H5 • 3 km (2 miles) west of Phaestos • 28920 91564 • 9:30am–4:30pm daily • Adm; also combined ticket with Phaestos (pp20–21)*

10 Boutari Winery and Audio-Visual Show

At the Fantaxometochi Winery, south of Knosos near Archanes village, one of Greece's leading winemakers has opened a state-of-the-art audiovisual show celebrating the island – its landscapes, history and traditional way of life. The show also highlights the vineyards and grape varieties that produce some of the Boutari family's award-winning wines. You can sample and buy Boutari red and white wines at the winery shop. ⊗ *Map K4 • 28107 31617 • 9am–5pm Mon–Fri, visits by appt on weekends (Nov–Mar: 8:30am–4:30pm) • Adm • www.boutari.gr*

The lower slopes of Mt Idi

Left **The harbour** Right **The Venetian Arsenal**

🔟 A Morning in Irakleio

Porta Kenouria
The most appropriate place to start exploring Irakleio's Venetian heritage is this ornate archway through the city's mighty walls, built in the mid-16th century by the Italian military engineer Michele Sanmichele. At this point, the walls are some 40 m (130 ft) thick, so it is not surprising that they withstood 16th-century Ottoman artillery and everything else thrown at them.

Pumphouse and Fountain
Walk through the portal and along Evans, named after the excavator of ancient Knosos, to Plateia Kornarou, named after the writer of the Cretan epic poem the *Erotokritos*. In the middle of this square stands a pretty, six-sided stone building, a café set within a pumphouse built by the Turks. Stop here, if you like, for a coffee in the shade of plane trees. Beside the café is the Venetian Bembo Fountain – note the broken, decapitated marble torso of a Roman statue built into its stonework.

Market stalls, Odos 1866

Market
Leave Plateia Kornarou north of the fountain, along the market street Odos 1866, among stalls selling fresh fruit, olives, dried fruit and nuts, and less familiar produce such as buckets of live snails. Midway along 1866, turn left and walk along to Plateia Ekaterinis, where the main landmark is the pompous 19th-century cathedral.

Agia Ekaterini
In the 16th century, this church was one of the great schools of Cretan icon painting. While the icon museum is closed today, the church remains open to the public. Many of the icons have been moved to the church of Agios Minas.

Plateia Venizelou
Leave Plateia Ekaterinis by its northwest corner, and walk east to Plateia Nikoforou Foka, then left to Plateia Venizelou. The Morosini fountain

Venetian fountain

For more on Irakleio See pp12–15 & p80

Left **Agia Ekaterini** Right **Venetian Fortress**

stands in the middle of the square, with two stone lions standing sentinel.

San Marco and the Loggia
On the square's southeast side, the former Venetian Cathedral of San Marco, dedicated to Venice's patron saint, became a mosque and is now an exhibition centre and conference hall. Leave the square by 25 Augoustou, passing the Loggia. If this Venetian town hall looks suspiciously modern, blame restoration after earthquake and bomb damage.

Agios Titos
Turn right immediately after the Loggia to find Agios Titos (St Titus). Originally Byzantine, the church was rebuilt by the Venetians, turned into a mosque by the Turks and reclaimed by the Orthodox church in 1925. Inside, a reliquary contains the skull of St Titus. ◎ *8am–8pm daily • Free*

Historical Museum
Returning to 25 Augoustou, turn left onto Theotokopoulou, then left onto Gazi, which leads to the Historical Museum of Crete. The basement contains some interesting Venetian stonework, Turkish and Byzantine remnants and the only El Greco painting left in Crete. ◎ *28102 83219 • 9am–5pm Mon–Sat (winter: to 3:30pm) • Adm • www.historical-museum.gr*

Venetian Fortress
Built in 1523–40 to guard the harbour approaches, the massive Rocca al Mare, as it was known to the Venetians, served its purpose well. Piles of cannonballs in the inner chambers seem to await another assault. ◎ *28102 46299 • Closed for renovation; expected to reopen in 2016 – call for updates*

Venetian Arsenal (Arsenali)
On the way back from the fortress is a series of high stone vaults built into the wall behind the harbour. These were the Arsenali, or shipyards, where the great galleys that gave Venice its control of the sea were built.

Agios Titos

Flavour of the Walk
Crete's bustling capital has a wealth of relics of its Venetian past tucked away in nooks and corners among its more modern buildings. Start this walk as early as you can – Irakleio becomes uncomfortably hot by early afternoon. Allow three to four hours.

Following pages **Nida Plateau and Mt Idi**

Left **Chersonisos resort** Right **Agia Galini beach**

Beaches

1 Malia
A long strip of bars, clubs, shops, hotels and apartments lines the main coast highway at Malia. The splendid sandy beach is crowded with sun loungers and umbrellas from early summer until September. ⊗ *Map M4*

2 Chersonisos
A big, brash resort that may soon grow to merge with neighbouring Stalida and Malia. The beach is unarguably superb, and has an array of multinational bars and restaurants. ⊗ *Map L3*

3 Matala
A series of sandy coves separated by rocky headlands, Matala first attracted sun-seeking hippy travellers in the 1960s and graduated to become a small holiday resort in the 1980s. ⊗ *Map G6*

4 Agia Galini
On a crescent bay where a reed-lined river meets the sea, this is a classic fishing village turned beach resort. ⊗ *Map G5*

5 Bali
A small, purpose-built resort set around three coves sheltered by cliffs. Avoid the crowds from June to September. ⊗ *Map H3*

6 Dytikos (Lendas)
One of the longest beaches on the south central coast, Dytikos is popular with nudist sunbathers. ⊗ *Map J6*

7 Kato Gouves (Gouvia)
With its long stretch of sand and shingle and growing number of package holiday hotels, this is one of the better beaches close to Irakleio. ⊗ *Map L3*

8 Panormos
One of the less developed beaches on the central north coast, Panormos has a small sandy beach beside a miniature fishing harbour and a few places to eat and drink. ⊗ *Map G3*

9 Kaloi Limenes
A relatively remote and peaceful series of small beaches and coves among dramatic cliffs. But the offshore oil tanker terminal rather mars the view. ⊗ *Map H6*

10 Irakleio
If you have time to kill while in the capital, head for the municipal beach at Amnisos, which is open from 9am to 7pm for a small fee. ⊗ *Map K3*

Matala

Left **Malia beach** Right **Palace of Malia**

🔟 Best of the Rest

1 Museum of Cretan Ethnology, Vori
One of the first museums to celebrate the lives of ordinary Cretans (see p38).

2 Palace of Malia
Only 3 km (2 miles) inland from the bustling resort of modern Malia, a ruined Minoan palace seems to grow from the rocky hillside (see pp34–5).

3 Mt Giouchtas
Looming to the south of Archanes, Mt Giouchtas is the mythical burial place of the god Zeus. The remains of a Minoan sanctuary are below the summit, and the area has been declared a conservation area, with the aim of protecting eagles, vultures and other raptors. ❧ Map K4

4 Minoan Villa Site, Tylissos
Tylissos was inhabited more than 4,000 years ago, but the most interesting discoveries are the remains of three large Minoan villas. ❧ Map J4 • 28102 26470 • 9am–4pm daily • Adm

5 Archanes Archaeological Museum
The small farming town of Archanes has a surprisingly good museum with finds from nearby sites, including clay Minoan coffins, fragments of pottery, and a sacrificial dagger that may have been used in human sacrifice. ❧ Map K4 • 28107 52712 • 8am–3pm Wed–Mon • Adm

6 Church of Agios Mikhail Arkhangelos, Asomatos
The Archangel Michael, leader of the heavenly host, is known in Greek as "O Taxiarchis" (the Brigadier) and is depicted in armour, sword in hand, along with other saints in the frescoes within the pretty 14th-century church at Asomatos. ❧ Map K4

7 Koudouma Monastery
The monks of Koudouma live in enviable isolation in a tiny monastery on a sandy beach fringed with palm trees. ❧ Map J6 • Dawn to dusk daily • Donations welcome

8 Minoan Villa Site, Vathypetrou
Vathypetrou was presumably the home of a Minoan landowner, and ancient wine-making equipment found on the site indicates that the surrounding vineyards are thousands of years old. ❧ Map K4 • 28102 26470 • 8:30am–3pm Tue–Sun • Free

9 Mt Kofinas
A mere hillock by Cretan standards, but still a challenging climb (starting from Kapetaniana village) with great views of Mt Idi (see p53) and the south coast.

10 Cretaquarium, Irakleio
Situated just a 10-minute drive from Irakleio airport, this aquarium is home to 2,500 individual sea-creatures from 200 Mediterranean species. ❧ Map K4 • 28103 37788 • 9:30am–5pm daily (May–Sep: to 9pm) • Adm • www.cretaquarium.gr

Left **Street with tavernas, Agia Galini** Right **New York bar, Chersonisos**

TOP 10 Bars and Cafés

1 Mare, Irakleio
Located on the waterfront, Mare serves coffee and light snacks by day and cocktails by night. Enjoy the sunset on the café's lovely terrace. ✆ *Sofokli Venizelou • Map S1 • 2810 41946*

2 The Four Lions, Irakleio
Open from early morning until late at night, this rooftop café offers a panoramic view of the older part of Irakleio. It has cold drinks, snacks, wines, spirits and cocktails. ✆ *Plateia Venizelou • Map T2*

3 Kirkor, Irakleio
Start the day with a Cretan-style breakfast of coffee and a cream-filled pastry while enjoying the view of the Lion Fountain. ✆ *Liontara Square • Map T1*

4 Pagopoieion, Irakleio
Set in the city's old ice factory, this interesting café-bar serves Greek, Italian and iced coffees all day long. The decor includes mementoes of the building's past, including the old ice lift. ✆ *Platia Agios Titos • Map T2 • 28103 46028*

To Petrino, Agia Galini

5 Korais, Irakleio
This glitzy, open-air café-bar has overhead movie screens and music playing on its flowery terraces, making it popular with the fashionable local crowd. ✆ *Korai 3 • Map T2 • 28103 46336*

6 C'est La Vie Bar, Agia Galini
Enjoy breakfast, coffee, drinks and ice cream at this bar with a picturesque view of the harbour. ✆ *In the harbour • Map G5 • 28320 91113*

7 Acropol, Matala
Try one of the 12 breakfasts or a dish of fresh fruit and yogurt at this café with a typical Greek atmosphere. ✆ *Behind the Matala Bay Hotel • Map G6 • 28920 45396*

8 Port Side, Matala
This cocktail bar is above the beach and has great views of the bay. Coffee and snacks are served all day. ✆ *Above the beach • Map G6 • 694 5983 886*

9 New York, Chersonisos
On the beach close to the harbour entrance, enjoy break-fast, snacks and cold drinks at this beach bar during the day and party to the lively music at night. ✆ *Map L3 • 28970 23415*

10 To Petrino, Agia Galini
An old-fashioned café and ouzeri, To Petrino serves break-fast, coffee and tasty meze with local wines and beer. ✆ *Off the harbour platia • Map G5 • 28320 91504*

For more restaurants, tavernas, bars, cafés and ouzeries
See pp68–73

Price Categories

For a three-course		
meal for one with half	€	under €12
a bottle of wine (or	€€	€12–€18
equivalent meal), taxes	€€€	€18–€24
and extra charges.	€€€€	€24–€32
	€€€€€	over €32

Left **Loukoulos restaurant, Irakleio**

Restaurants

Loukoulos, Irakleio
Probably the best restaurant in Irakleio serves Italian cuisine in upmarket surroundings (white linen tablecloths and candles in the evening) in a room with antique prints and paintings. ◈ *Korai 5 • Map T2 • 2810 224435 • €€€€€*

I Erganos, Irakleio
Hearty Cretan cooking in a family-run place. Specials include *sygouri* (meat soup) and a selection of grilled meat dishes.
◈ *Georgiadou 5 • 2810 285629 • €€*

O Kyriakos, Irakleio
In traditional taverna style, you will be beckoned into the kitchen of this old-fashioned restaurant with smoke-stained, wood-panelled walls to choose your meal from bubbling pots or glass cases filled with fish, chops and vegetables. ◈ *Leoforos Dimokratias 53 • 2810 222464 • €€*

Kipos Ton Gefseon, Irakleio
Housed in a stylish old villa, this restaurant offers traditional Cretan food. You can eat indoors or in the lovely garden surrounded by trees. ◈ *Chrisostomou Av. 8 • Map K3 • 28103 00358 • €€€*

Brillant, Irakleio
A stylish gourmet restaurant attached to the Lato Boutique Hotel, Brilliant serves Cretan cuisine with a twist. The views of the harbour and the Venetian fortress are stunning. ◈ *Epimenidou 15 • Map T1 • 28103 34959 • €€€€€*

Aetos, Anogeia
A traditional village taverna, this restaurant's speciality is lamb and goat barbecued on a wood-fired grill. They also serve a variety of excellent local cheeses. ◈ *Upper village • Map H4 • 28340 31262 • €€*

Tria Adelfia, Chersonisos
Enjoy traditional dancing in the main square from this authentic and reasonably priced Greek taverna serving local delicacies. ◈ *Main Square, Old Chersonisos • Map L4 • €€€€*

El Greco, Lendas
A traditional Greek taverna overlooking the Libyan Sea, El Greco offers fine traditional food made with local ingredients and an extensive wine list with plenty of local choices. ◈ *Above the beach • Map J6 • 28920 95322 • €€€€*

Erotokritos, Ammoudara
This taverna serves traditional Cretan appetizers and main courses. Its white wine from the barrel is particularly good.
◈ *Papandreou 109 • Map K3 • 28102 52426 • Noon–midnight all year • €€*

Taverna Agios Ioannis, Agios Ioannis
Close to the archaeological site at Phaestos, this rural taverna's house speciality is rabbit *(kouneli)*, served at tables set under a vine-shaded trellis.
◈ *Main road just outside the village • Map G5 • 28920 42006 • €€€*

Left **Firkas Fort, Chania** Centre **Market stall, Rethymno** Right **The beach at Rethymno**

Western Crete

WESTERN CRETE IS IN MANY WAYS *the most exciting part of the island. Much of the west is dominated by the jagged, treeless peaks of the Lefka Ori (White Mountains), which may be capped by snow until June. Traversed by gorges, the mountains drop sharply to the Libyan Sea on Crete's south coast. These mountains were for centuries the heartland of Cretan resistance to foreign occupiers of the island. Many of the remoter villages were accessible only on foot until the second half of the 20th century, and a traditional way of life lingered longer here than in other parts of the island. The west also has Crete's two most attractive towns, Chania and Rethymno, and some of the best beaches, ranging from pebbly coves to long swathes of golden sand.*

Sights in Western Crete

1	Rethymno	**6**	Sougia
2	Chania	**7**	Loutro
3	Samaria Gorge	**8**	Georgioupoli
4	Paleochora	**9**	Plakias
5	Frangokastello	**10**	Kastelli Kissamou

Villager, Sougia

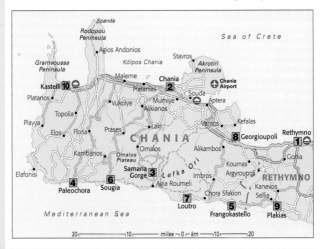

Chania harbour

1 Rethymno

Rethymno is Crete's third largest town (after Irakleio and Chania) and its most attractive, with an inner harbour overlooked by a huge, brooding Venetian fortress (the Fortetsa), streets of old-fashioned Venetian mansions, and a palm-fringed esplanade along a sandy beach. Thanks to its nearby beaches, Rethymno has become a fully fledged resort town, with holiday hotels east of the city centre, and lots of shops, restaurants, bars and cafés. It also has a colourful early morning market on Thursday and Saturday (see pp22–3 & pp94–5).

2 Chania

Chania, Crete's second largest city, is built around a fine natural harbour which attracted a host of settlers over the millennia, from early Minoans to Romans, Byzantines, Saracens, Venetians and Turks. The heart of the city is the old town, a huddle of narrow streets sheltered by a ring of battlements built by the Venetians; under their rule Chania was one of Crete's most important ports. Today the old town is dominated by restaurants, cafés and bars, while outside the Venetian walls is the newer part of town. Chania has some of Crete's

Nerandzes Mosque, Rethymno

most spectacular scenery as backdrop, with the slopes of the Lefka Ori range (White Mountains) rising steeply a short way inland and seeming to dominate the entire southern horizon (see pp18–19).

3 Samaria Gorge

Taking its name from the tiny Venetian church of Santa Maria (close to the now abandoned Samaria village), this is probably the most dramatic stretch of scenery in Crete. The gorge is one of the deepest and longest in Europe, cutting its way through the Lefka Ori from the Omalos Plateau to the Libyan Sea, and narrowing to a width of only a few arm widths at its narrowest point. The gorge is within the Samaria National Park, a refuge for many rare birds, plants and mammals (see pp26–7).

Samaria Gorge

Paleochora

Paleochora

4 Paleochora stands on a peninsula between two beaches: a long sandy bay to the northwest and an even longer, but pebblier and more exposed beach, to the southeast. Close to the centre of the village are the ruined walls of a Venetian fort, Castel Selino, which was built to guard the harbour and coast but left to crumble after the Turkish conquest. "Discovered" by backpackers in the 1970s, Paleochora is now one of Crete's quieter resorts, with a low-key nightlife and a family atmosphere. ✪ *Map B4*

Frangokastello

5 A small, deserted "Castle of the Franks" – actually built in 1371 by the Venetians to defend this stretch of the south coast against pirate attacks *(see p40)* – gives this small fishing village and resort its name. The Lion of St Mark, symbol of the Venetian Republic, still adorns the town's southern gateway. Frangokastello has a long sweep of grey sandy beach, and offers, by way of accommodation, small pensions and apartments. A handful of restaurants and cafés open up in summer, but the choice of places to eat, drink and stay is very limited in the low season. ✪ *Map E4*

Bandit Country

The Sfakia region lived by its own fierce laws for generations, and vendettas between local families were not uncommon even a couple of generations back. Prosperity and communications have tamed the region somewhat, but many Sfakiots still have an illicit firearm or two (often of World War II vintage) hidden away in the attic – and in the remoter parts it seems that no road sign has escaped target practice.

Sougia

6 Sougia is perfect for anyone in search of peace, quiet and isolation. Tourism is very low-key, with just a scattering of small pensions and guest houses, tavernas and cafés. The town's beach is long and pebbly, and the water is sparklingly clear, while an hour's walk away are the ruins of the ancient city-state of Lissos, including a temple to Asklepios, the god of healing, which dates from the 3rd century BC. ✪ *Map C4*

Sougia beach

Left **Loutro** Right **Georgioupoli**

Loutro

Sheltered by a stretch of headland and dwarfed by the near-vertical slopes of the Lefka Ori (White Mountains) above it, Loutro is one of the most charming spots on Crete. Less than 30 years ago Loutro had only a few elderly inhabitants and one taverna. Tourism has changed all that, and now dazzling white pensions and apartments sit above the tiny crescent-shaped beach. Accessible only on foot (by a precarious cliff path) or by boat from Chora Sfakion, Loutro seems unlikely to be over-run by tourism, and is ideal for a laid-back holiday. ⊗ *Map D4*

Georgioupoli

A modern community by Cretan standards, the town was founded little over a century ago when it was named in honour of Prince George, the then governor of Crete. It is now a resort, with hotels stretching along the sandy beach. It attracts a less raucous clientele than resorts such as Malia and Chersonisos, however, and the heart of Georgioupoli is a town square, shaded by eucalyptus and plane trees. ⊗ *Map E3*

Plakias

Plakias is one of Crete's newer resorts. Its excellent beaches were overlooked by the holiday industry until the 1990s, at which point, the tiny fishing and farming community began to transform into a strip of purpose-built hotels (none of them obtrusively large), apartments, shops and restaurants. Not for those looking for authenticity, Plakias nevertheless has plenty going for it, including attractive surrounding countryside, its own long sweep of shingly sand, and lots more even prettier beaches and palm-fringed coves within walking distance. ⊗ *Map F4*

Kastelli Kissamou

Usually known simply as Kastelli, Crete's westernmost town is couched in a bay between the Rodopou and Gramvoussa peninsulas. It has largely missed out on the tourism boom, although it has a handful of hotels and restaurants. There are several rarely visited ancient and medieval sites nearby, including the ruins of Polyrinia *(see p41)*, and there are reasonable – if unexceptional by Cretan standards – beaches on either side of town. ⊗ *Map B2*

Preveli beach, near Plakias

Left **Rimondi Fountain** Right **Folk Art Museum**

A Morning in Rethymno

Nerandzes Mosque

1 Porta Guora
Make an early start at Plateia Tessaron Martyron, the large square from which the Venetian Porta Guora – the only intact remnant of the Venetian city walls – leads into the old town. The Tessaron Martyron (Four Martyrs) Church at the northeast corner of the square honours four Cretans executed in 1824 by the Turks for remaining secretly Christian despite an apparent conversion to Islam. A pointed minaret by the church is all that is left of one of the city's Turkish mosques.

2 The Market
Passing through the gate, walk north on Ethnikis Antistasis, which bustles with produce stalls, small open-fronted shops and cafés serving tiny glasses of *raki* and cups of coffee. This is a great place to buy Cretan herbs, honey or olive oil to take home.

3 Agios Frangiskos
Follow Ethnikis Antistasis north to the Church of Agios Frangiskos (St Francis), which was formerly part of a Venetian Roman Catholic monastery. The doorway is beautifully carved and the basilica is still used by the town's small Roman Catholic community.

4 Nerandzes Mosque
At the north end of Ethnikis Antistasis is the Nerandzes Mosque, the town's best preserved Ottoman relic dating back to the 17th century. It is now a music school and concert hall, and its slender, pointed minaret can be seen from some distance. It was previously a Catholic church dedicated to Santa Maria. Although the building has been fully restored, the original doorway remains.

Market flower stall

5 Historical and Folk Art Museum
Back at street level, turn left onto Vernardou and, midway along on your left, step into the Historical and Folk Art Museum, with its collection of tools, textiles and traditional costume *(see also p22).* ◈ 28 Vernardou • 10am–2:30pm Mon–Sat • Adm

For more on Rethymno, see pp22–23 & p91

Rethymno harbour

Venetian Loggia

This elegant 16th-century loggia is a poignant reminder of Venice's reign. The visible walls have equal semi-circular arches, with the middle one serving as the entrance to the ground floor. It is now a museum and art gallery *(see also p23)*. ◉ *Palaiológou & Arkadiou • Mar–Sep daily • Adm*

Rimondi Fountain

Turn right again on Arabatzoglou, which leads down to Petihaki, a small square crammed with cafés. Stop for a drink and snack at Zanafoti, an old-fashioned café close to the 17th-century Rimondi Fountain, built in 1627 to supply part of the old town with fresh drinking water.

Rethymno Archaeological Museum

From the square, bear left past the fountain, along Mesolongiou and Himaras, to the Rethymno Archaeological Museum, which displays Minoan coffins and burial goods, as well as Neolithic and Roman finds *(see also p36)*. ◉ *Cheimarras • 28310 54668 • 8am–3pm Tue–Sun • Adm*

The Fortetza

From the museum, cross Katehaki to the Fortetza, built in 1573 by the Venetians *(see also p22 & p40)*. This massive fortress was built in response to the threat of Turkish invasion, but in the end it proved no match for the might of the Ottoman Empire. ◉ *Katechaki • 28310 25101 • Summer: 8:30am–8:30pm daily; winter: call for opening timings • Adm*

Venetian Harbour

Conclude your tour down at the pretty Venetian (or Inner) Harbour, and treat yourself to a seafood lunch at one of the numerous tavernas lining the quayside. ◉ *Nearchou 45*

Fortetza

Flavour of the Walk

Built by the Venetians, Rethymno's old quarter preserves a pleasantly old-fashioned air, with narrow streets and lanes lined with tall old stucco-fronted town houses. Venetian and Turkish drinking fountains are tucked away down side streets, and the domes and spires of the city's surviving mosques – now used for secular purposes – are reminders of its multi-cultural history. This walk around the old quarter takes no more than three hours.

Left **Falasarna** Right **Stavros**

🔟 Beaches

1 Preveli (Finikas)
The Kourtaliotis river meets the sea at Preveli, where the green river, blue sea, date palms and "Greek bamboo" (calamus reeds) create a tropical oasis feel. ◈ *Map F5*

2 Falasarna
This long sweep of yellow sand is one of the finest on the west coast, and has yet to be exploited by the tourist industry – though there are a few places to stay. ◈ *Map A2*

3 Platanias
The best beach within easy reach of Chania, and the village has plenty of places to eat and drink. This is Chania's after-dark summer playground, with pubs, clubs and discos. ◈ *Map C2*

4 Stavros
Quieter than Platanias, and so an attractive alternative for those seeking a little tranquillity. The lagoon-like bay featured in the film *Zorba the Greek*. ◈ *Map D2*

5 Agios Pavlos
At the foot of the Samaria Gorge, and so perfect for a

Platanias

restorative swim in its cool waters after the downhill hike. ◈ *Map D4*

6 Elafonisi
The superb beach opposite the island of Elafonisi on the west coast is one of Crete's best, with a long crescent of white sand and shallow turquoise water that warms up quickly in summer. Very busy. ◈ *Map A4*

7 Sougia
Shaded in places by a line of Tamarisk trees, Sougia's position between Paleochora and Agia Roumeli makes it ideal for a quick plunge for walkers treading a coastal route. ◈ *Map C4*

8 Marmara (Marble Beach)
A collection of sheltered coves lined with smooth white pebbles. Marmara attracts nude sunbathers and can be reached by boat from Loutro. ◈ *Map D4*

9 Glika Nera (Sweetwater Beach)
A tiny patch of pebble and sand reachable only by scrambling along a rocky cliff path, or by boat from Loutro or Chora Sfakion. Often used by nudists. ◈ *Map D4*

10 Damnoni
Its golden sands have been somewhat marred by insensitive hotel building, but east of the main beach are smaller sandy coves, Ammoudi and Skinaria. ◈ *Map F4*

Previous pages **Frangokastello**

Left **Chora Sfakion** Right **Archaia Eleftherna**

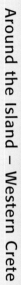

🔟 Best of the Rest

Moni Gonia, Rodopou Peninsula

Anogeia
Pleasant cafés and shops conceal Anogeia's embattled past, when it was a hotbed of resistance against the Turks, who sacked it in 1821 and 1826, and the Germans, who levelled it in 1944. ✆ *Map H4*

Chora Sfakion
A major rendezvous point for excursion groups who arrive by boat having walked the Samaria Gorge. Once they have found their coaches, the town returns to its pleasant slumber. ✆ *Map D4*

Archaia Eleftherna
Founded in 700 BC, ancient Eleftherna was a powerful Dorian city. Having vanished from history, it is now being rediscovered by archaeologists. ✆ *Map G3 • 8.30am–7pm daily • Free*

Polyrinia
Wonderful views surround the broken walls and foundations of this ancient Acropolis, upon which stands an equally ruined Venetian fortress *(see p41)*.

Monastery of Agia Irini
This restored 14th-century monastery is now a nunnery and also a centre for traditional weaving and needlework. ✆ *Map F3 • 28310 27791 • 9am–8pm daily*

Aptera
A Byzantine town built on the site of a Hellenistic city, remains here include Roman cisterns, Byzantine foundations, a Venetian monastery and a Turkish fort. ✆ *Map D2 • 8:30am–3pm Tue–Sun • Free*

Gramvoussa Peninsula
The remote and barely populated Gramvoussa Peninsula has one of Crete's best beaches at Falasarna, where there are also the scattered remains of a Hellenistic city. ✆ *Map B1–2*

Rodopou Peninsula
A barren peninsula that attracted the Orthodox monks who built the monastery of Moni Gonia, which has several fine icons. ✆ *Moni Gonia • Map B1–2 • 8am–12:30pm, 4–8pm daily*

Akrotiri Peninsula
Monks have been drawn to Crete's peninsulas – Akrotiri's best monasteries are the abandoned Moni Katholikou and the Venetian Moni Gouverneto *(see p42)*.

Souda Bay War Cemetery
The burial place of more than 1,500 Allied soldiers who died during the Battle of Crete, in May 1941. ✆ *Map D2*

Left **Alcanea, Chania** Centre **Synagogi Bar, Chania** Right **Kafeneion O Platanos, Rethymno**

TOP 10 Bars and Cafés

1 Alcanea, Chania
A tranquil terrace café at the western tip of the harbour near the Naval Museum, Alcanea serves snacks, coffee, cocktails and wines. ◎ *Angelou 2 • Map A5 • 28210 75370*

2 Synagogi Bar, Chania
This popular bar is set in the large courtyard of a Venetian ruin that was once a synagogue. Cosy corner sofas and quiet music provide a low-key atmosphere. ◎ *12 Skoufon St, Old Harbour • Map A5*

3 Chocolat, Rethymno
Located opposite the marina, this outdoor café serves delicious pastries, cakes and ice creams, with chocolate being the predominant flavour. ◎ *S. Venizelou 3 • Map Q2 • 28310 53853*

4 Mylos, Platanias
A popular beachside club, Mylos has a bar and café serving refreshments. ◎ *Platanias Beach • Map C2 • 28210 60449*

5 Raki Bar Pandelis, Sougia
Old-fashioned wooden chairs, marble-topped tables and a vine-covered verandah are part of the appeal. Its interior – a vaulted bar with a wooden floor, set in an old stone building – is attractive too. ◎ *Sougia • Map C4*

Kafeneion Yannis, Paleochora

6 Kafeneion O Platanos, Rethymno
A rare authentic taverna, serving thimbles of Greek coffee and glasses of *tsikondia* (a strong spirit) to a clientele of venerable locals. ◎ *Plateia Petihaki • Map Q2*

7 Meli, Rethymno
Take a break from the heat of the day and enjoy delicious cake and superb ice cream at one of Meli's shady outdoor tables. ◎ *E. Venizelou 7 • Map Q2*

8 Cul de Sac, Rethymno
Close to the Rimondi Fountain on Rethymno's busiest square, Cul de Sac is the perfect place for people-watching over a coffee or a cocktail. ◎ *Plateia Petihaki • Map Q2 • 28310 26914*

9 Kafeneion Yannis, Paleochora
A traditional ouzeri on the town's main street. Don't expect a list of sophisticated cocktails; do expect an authentic Cretan ambience. ◎ *Odos Venizelos • Map B4*

10 Nostos Disco Bar, Paleochora
This is the best of the music bars along Pebble Beach. Rock, pop and the latest dance music is occasionally interspersed with Cretan dancing to traditional *lyra* rhythms. ◎ *Pebble Beach • Map B4 • 69748 93355*

For more restaurants, tavernas, bars, cafés and ouzeries See pp68–73

Price Categories

For a three-course meal for one with half a bottle of wine (or equivalent meal), taxes and extra charges.

€ under €12
€€ €12–€18
€€€ €18–€24
€€€€ €24–€32
€€€€€ over €32

Left **Kyria Maria, Rethymno**

🔟 Restaurants

1 Portes, Chania
Known for its adventurous cooking, Portes adds a twist to age-old favourites such as pork fillet stuffed with chestnuts or traditional pies with unexpected fillings.
◈ *Portou 48 • Map A6 • 28210 76261 • €€€€*

Veneto, Rethymno

2 Kariatis, Chania
This renowned Italian restaurant serves a wide variety of tasty dishes in beautiful surroundings among Venetian ruins.
◈ *12 Katehaki Sq, Old Harbour • Map B5 • 28210 55600 • From 7pm • €€€€€*

3 Tamam, Chania
A wide range of Greek, Cretan and Levantine dishes, with a better choice of non-meat dishes than most of its rivals. ◈ *49 Zambeliou • Map B5 • 28210 96080 • €€€*

4 Plateia, Mirthios
Traditional Cretan food, friendly staff and breathtaking views of the sea guarantee a good time at this restaurant.
◈ *Mirthios village • Map F4 • 28320 31560 • €€€*

5 Veneto, Rethymno
Set in 13th-century vaults beneath the Veneto Hotel, this restaurant serves Cretan specialities within a beautiful setting, with stone-flagged floors, mosaics and antique furniture.
◈ *4 Epimenidou • 28310 56634 • €€€€€*

6 Avli, Rethymno
One of the town's finest eateries serves grilled and roasted meats and Cretan dishes such as *apatzia* sausages and roasted goat in a garden setting. ◈ *22 Xanthoudidou • Map Q2 • 28310 26213 • €€€€*

7 Kyria Maria, Rethymno
This little taverna in the old quarter serves plain, village-style dishes. It gets busy in the evenings. ◈ *20 Moschovitou • Map Q2 • 28310 29078 • Closed Nov–Mar • €€€*

8 Taverna tou Zisi, Rethymno
On the old Irakleio highway, 4 km (2 miles) east of Rethymno, Zisi's charcoal-grilled lamb and chicken are worth the short trip from town. ◈ *Missiria • 28310 28814 • €€€*

9 Kali Kardia, Kournas
Close to Crete's only lake, Kali Kardia offers simple yet delicious fare, almost all home-grown and organic. The sausages *(loukanika)* are locally renowned and the lamb is excellent too.
◈ *Kournas village • Map E3 • 28250 96278 • €€€*

10 Sterna tou Bloumosifi, Vamos
Part of a restored 19th-century stone village, this taverna serves Cretan specialities baked in wood-burning ovens. ◈ *Vamos • Map E2 • €€€*

Left **Ancient bath, Archaeological Museum, Agios Nikolaos** Centre **Siteia** Right **Market, Siteia**

Eastern Crete

CRETE'S FAR EAST is a little less rugged than the wild west, and less populous than the central region of the island. It also sees rather fewer package holidaymakers, mainly because of its remoteness from the island's airports. That said, the region's largest town, Agios Nikolaos, is a thriving holiday resort, while Crete's most expensive and exclusive hotel and villa complexes can be found around Elounda, on the Gulf of Mirabello. The east also has good beaches, on its north, south and east coasts, notably the famous palm beach at Vai, and there are Minoan ruins to be seen at Gournia, Mochlos, Zakros and elsewhere.

Sights in Eastern Crete

1. Agios Nikolaos
2. Siteia
3. Vai
4. Zakros Gorge
5. Elounda
6. Makrygialos
7. Spinalonga
8. Ierapetra
9. Lato
10. Mochlos

Agios Nikolaos

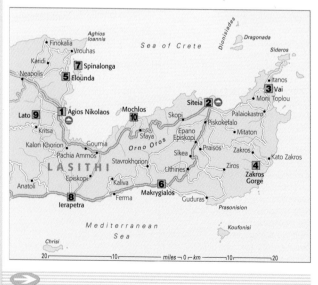

Agios Nikolaos harbour

1 Agios Nikolaos

Agios Nikolaos has the most attractive location of any town in eastern Crete. By the Gulf of Mirabello, it is built around an inner lagoon, Voulismeni, which is surrounded by palm trees and cafés. Modern hotels and apartments dwarf the surviving older buildings, but it is still a place of considerable charm. There is a small town beach, and boats take holiday-makers to larger beaches nearby. The town takes its name from the tiny 11th-century church of Agios Nikolaos (which now stands in the grounds of the Minos Palace Hotel). The Archaeological Museum (see pp36–7) displays numerous finds from nearby sites including Mochlos and Gournia. ✎ Map N4

2 Siteia

Siteia looks surprisingly modern but was founded in the 4th century, when a flourishing Byzantine city stood here. Its fortunes waned after the 14th century, when it was damaged by earthquakes and sacked by corsairs. It was not until the late 19th century that Siteia became an important farming centre, surrounded by olive groves and vineyards. It has a picturesque harbour overlooked by a Venetian fortress and an Archaeological Museum (see p36). Siteia is becoming an important area for the production of quality Cretan wines. ✎ Map Q4

3 Vai

The main claim to fame of the beach at Vai is in having the only wild palm grove in Europe. The palm forest apparently existed at least 2,000 years ago, so may have been planted by early navigators from the Middle East who came to Crete. The drawbacks are that the palm trees are fenced off and protected, and the beach becomes overrun with visitors in high season. Nevertheless, it is beautiful, especially if visited outside the busiest summer months of June, July and August. ✎ Map R4

Vai

Left **Zakros Gorge** Right **A beachside taverna, Kato Zakros**

Zakros Gorge
The Zakros Gorge is known locally as the Valley of the Dead because the numerous caves in its limestone walls were used as tombs in Roman times. The gorge runs from the peaceful village of Ano ("upper") Zakros to Kato ("lower") Zakros on the sea, near an ancient Minoan palace site rediscovered in 1961. It is a beautiful and not too challenging 8-km (5-mile) hike (see also p53). ✎ Map Q5

Elounda
Elounda, on the Gulf of Mirabello, is Crete's most expensive resort area, with several exclusive villa and hotel complexes in landscaped grounds. Several of these even have private beaches. The village itself is less up-market, with a clutter of shops and restaurants surrounding a small fishing harbour from which boats depart daily in summer on

The Caves of Crete

About 5,000 caverns and potholes riddle the island's mountain slopes. Grottoes have yielded fascinating relics of the ancient world, indicating that Crete was inhabited for thousands of years before the rise of the Minoan civilization. Only a handful have been fully charted, and thousands more remain to be fully explored and mapped.

trips to Spinalonga, the Venetian fortress-island and former leper colony not far offshore. ✎ Map N4

Makrygialos
Makrygialos is the most popular holiday resort on the southeast coast, with a long, straggling array of small pensions, hotels and tavernas stretching along a crescent of rather wind-swept, gently shelving sand and pebble beach, which is the best in this part of the island. ✎ Map P5

Spinalonga
The fortifications covering this small, rocky island in the Gulf of Mirabello were built by the Venetians in 1579 to control the approaches to this superb natural

Elounda harbour

For the archaeological site of Gournia see pp30–31

harbour. Superior sea power allowed Venice to hang onto Spinalonga for half a century after the fall of the rest of Crete to the Turks, and it was surrendered only in 1715. Used as a leper colony in the first half of the 20th century, its buildings are now very dilapidated, but the grim walls may still give the visitor an eerie thrill.  Map N4

Ruins on Spinalonga

Ierapetra

Ierapetra is the largest town on the southeast coast. Its buildings are rather dull, but it has a good, long beach of grey sand and the distinction of receiving more hours of sunshine per year than anywhere else in Europe. Huge crops of tomatoes are raised all year round in the surrounding farmlands. Ierapetra became an important Dorian Greek settlement as early as the 8th century BC, and by the 2nd century BC, it was the largest city-state on the island after defeating its Eteocretan neighbours, Praisos and Itanos. Under the Romans, it was an important seaport; the Venetians built a fortress to defend the harbour. Map N6

Myrtos beach, near Ierapetra

Lato

Modern-day Agios Nikolaos was once no more than the seaport annex of this Dorian Greek city which flourished between the 7th and 3rd centuries BC. Built around two neighbouring hills, 8 km (5 miles) west of Agios Nikolaos, Lato is the best preserved Dorian site in Crete, with walls built of massive stone blocks. There are fine views over the Gulf of Mirabello from its *agora* (market-place) in a saddle between the twin summits. Map M4
• 8am–3pm Tue–Sun • Adm

Mochlos

Mochlos, 32 km (20 miles) east of Agios Nikolaos on the coast road, is a tiny fishing hamlet with a handful of tavernas. Just offshore is the island of Mochlos, which in ancient times was connected to the mainland by an isthmus. This has been eroded by earthquakes and waves. On the island are the remains of Minoan houses and a Minoan harbour, much of which is now under water. Seal stones, superb gold jewellery and vases carved from quartz, alabaster and black steatite have been discovered in rock tombs on the island and are displayed in the Agios Nikolaos and Siteia arch-aeological museums. Map P4

Left **Ancient steps, Gournia** Centre **Boat near Vai** Right **Heron, Zakros**

A Day's Drive in Eastern Crete

1 Gournia
Early in the morning, on any day except a Monday, head east out of Agios Nikolaos on the main island highway. Gournia is south of the road, 24 km (15 miles) east of Agios Nikolaos. Try to arrive when it opens at 8:30am and allow a couple of hours to explore this well preserved Minoan site *(see pp30–31)*. ◈ Map N5

2 Mochlos
Leaving Gournia, drive on along the coast highway to Mochlos, 11 km (7 miles) east of Gournia. This tiny fishing hamlet has a handful of tavernas, and a small boat will take you to the pretty island where the foundations of Minoan houses can be seen. ◈ Map P4

3 Siteia
Once a Byzantine city, Siteia was destroyed in the 14th century, then rebuilt by a local *pasha* (Ottoman governor) in the late 19th century *(see p103)*. It has a picturesque harbour overlooked by a Venetian fortress and an Archaeological Museum with Minoan treasures. Stop for coffee, a cold drink or a snack at Zorbas, an old-fashioned café and taverna on the harbour *(see p113)*. ◈ Map Q4

4 Moni Toplou
A 10-km (6-mile) drive from Siteia takes you along the north coast to Moni Toplou, a fortified monastery founded in the 14th century, with sturdy stone walls around an inner courtyard with three tiers of tiny monks' cells. Its small church holds some remarkable icons, including one of the finest in Crete, *Lord Thou Art Great*, by Ioannis Kornaros *(see also p57)*. ◈ Map Q4

5 Vai
A further 6 km (4 miles) brings you to Vai *(see p103)*, the easternmost point of this drive, on a peninsula which stretches towards Crete's northeast tip (inaccessible as it is a military area). Vai's famous palm forest is now a conservation area. The beach is very crowded in high

Harbour life, Siteia

Left **Vai beach** Right **Ierapetra harbour**

season, but for a little more seclusion you can walk for 20–30 minutes to the less crowded coves at Itanos. ◈ *Map R4*

Zakros

After visiting Vai, turn south, through the small villages of Palaiokastro, Azokeramos, Adravasti and Ano Zakros, where you turn east for 8 km (5 miles) down a narrow road to reach Kato Zakros, on the sea. Stop here for lunch at one of the beachside tavernas. If you have the time and inclination, explore the Minoan palace *(see p35)*. ◈ *Map Q5*

Praisos

From Kato Zakros, retrace your tracks as far as Ano Zakros, then drive for 18 km (11 miles) through the villages of Ziros and Chandras to the ancient site at Praisos *(see p35)*. ◈ *Map Q5*

Lithines

Rejoin the main road and drive south for 8 km (5 miles) to the village of Lithines, built by tenants of the aristocratic Lithinos family in about the 10th century AD. Now a ghost village, it has two fine 15th-century churches. ◈ *Map Q5*

Makrygialos

The south coast of Crete is now only 10 km (6 miles) away. Stop for a late afternoon swim at Makrygialos, a popular beach resort with the best beach in this part of the island. Either stay here for your evening meal or continue to Ierapetra. ◈ *Map P5*

Ierapetra

It is a 45-minute drive to Ierapetra, the largest town on the southeast coast, passing rank on rank of greenhouses, which produce bumper crops of tomatoes, peppers and cucumbers. Ierapetra – originally named Ierapytna – was Crete's most important Dorian Greek city in the 2nd century BC *(see p105)*. Unlike most Cretan towns, Ierapetra is still more interested in farming than in the package holiday business and is a good place to glimpse everyday life on Crete. From here, it's a 32-km (20-mile) evening drive back to Agios Nikolaos. ◈ *Map N6*

Flavour of the Tour

This round trip from Agios Nikolaos covers around 200 km (125 miles). Allow one full day to give yourself time to explore the archaeological site at Gournia and to stop off at some of the other places mentioned. Roads are mostly well surfaced, and traffic is light. All sights and stops along the way are well signposted (in Greek and English).

Left **Siteia** Centre **Xerocampos** Right **Mirthios**

Beaches

Vai
Vai's beach is certainly the most scenic in eastern Crete, with yellow sand and a grove of date palms giving it a truly tropical appearance. ◈ Map R4

Siteia
Unlike most larger Cretan coastal towns, Siteia has a perfectly good beach right on its doorstep that is great for windsurfing. ◈ Map Q4

Xerocampos
A tiny village with a series of small, sandy east-facing coves, one of the few coast places not yet discovered by the package tourism industry. ◈ Map Q5

Kato Zakros
At the foot of the Zakros Gorge, Kato Zakros has a crescent of sand and pebble beach, with a small fishing harbour and a handful of pensions and tavernas. ◈ Map R5

Makrygialos
The best beach on the southeast coast. A long strip of

Mirthios
An amiably unpretentious farming and fishing village with a long, south-facing shingle beach, which is far less crowded than most in eastern Crete, even in high summer. ◈ Map M6

Kouremenos
Kouremenos is less than ideal for sunbathing because of strong breezes for most of the year. Those same breezes, however, make it a favourite windsurfing spot, with best conditions in summer usually in the afternoon. ◈ Map R4

Chionia
Rates a European Blue Flag for clean sand and water. There are even better, more secluded beaches to the south. ◈ Map R4

Milatos
A pebbly beach and surprisingly uncrowded compared with the teeming resorts only a few kilometres to the west. ◈ Map M4

sand interspersed with pebbles shelves gently into deeper water. ◈ Map P5

Istro
Looks spectacular from a distance, with a sandy beach hemmed in by cliffs. But it is often heavily littered with flotsam and jetsam. ◈ Map N5

Beachside taverna, Kato Zakros

Previous pages **A typical taverna-lined harbourfront**

Left **Handwoven rugs, Kritsa** Centre **Lithines** Right **Moni Kapsa**

🔟 Other Attractions

Praisos
Based on clay statuettes and inscriptions found here, archaeologists believe it was a post-Minoan Eteocretan city *(see p35)*.

Moni Toplou
Fortified monastery founded in the 14th century. Its massive walls were built to protect it from pirates *(see p42)*.

Pelekita Cave, Kato Zakros
Just 2 km (1.5 miles) northeast of Kato Zakros village and a few hundred metres north of the Zakros Gorge *(see p104)*, the Pelekita cavern is one of the longest in Crete. Map R5

Kritsa
Overlooked by Mt Kastelleos, Kritsa stands at the edge of a wide and fertile plain and is regarded as one of Crete's most important craft centres. Map M5

Itanos
Just north of Vai, Itanos has three small pebble and shingle beaches that are never as crowded as Vai's stretch of golden sand. The scant remains of an ancient city can be seen on the low hills beyond. Map R4

Rousa Eklisia
Pretty village worth visiting for its superb view of the bay. Large plane trees shade the village square, and a stream feeds a natural fountain next to an old church. Map Q5

Lithines
Named for its founders, the Litinos clan of Byzantine nobles, the village has two 15th-century churches, Agios Athanasios and Tis Panagias. Map Q5

Moni Kapsa
A monastery that seems to merge into the cliffs, with the mummified body of a monk in its chapel. Map Q6 • 8:30am–noon & 4–7pm

Pefki Gorge
A four-hour walk from Pefki to Makrygialos will take you along a dry river bed of white pebbles that runs through a canyon of weird rock formations. Map P5

Itanos

Voila
Deserted medieval village in rolling hill country, with a dilapidated Venetian tower standing guard over roofless cottages. The small church of Agios Georgios is well preserved. Map Q5

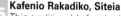

Café du Lac, Agios Nikolaos

Bars and Cafés

1 Café du Lac, Agios Nikolaos

Ices, cocktails, soft drinks, freshly squeezed orange juice and milk shakes are on the menu here. There is also an Internet café area. ◈ 28 Oktobriou 17 • Map N4

2 Puerto Bar, Agios Nikolaos

This stylish harbourfront café-bar provides great views from its terrace. Enjoy drinks and cocktails on the terrace during the day, then retreat indoors after dark as the music begins. ◈ Akti Koundourou 9 • Map N4 • 28410 23732

3 Kaaren's, Elounda

This café-bar has wonderful views of the sea and serves delicious sandwiches, wraps, homemade sausages and a wide range of cocktails. Not open for dinner. ◈ Akti Poseidonos • Map N4 • 28410 41709

4 Palm Beach, Vai

Located in a beautiful setting under palm trees on the beach, this café and snack bar offers coffee, drinks, nibbles and several flavours of ice cream prepared from fresh milk all day. ◈ On the beach • Map R4

5 Kafenio Rakadiko, Siteia

This traditional *kafeneion* is situated right on the waterfront, overlooking the harbour *(see p73)*. ◈ E. Venizelos 159 • Map Q4

6 Hellas, Elounda

A lively spot, with live Cretan music and Greek pop most weekends. ◈ Elounda village • Map N4 • Closed Nov–May

7 Veterano, Ierapetra

A fashionable terrace café ideal for a leisurely breakfast and just as good for a sundowner. ◈ Plateia Eleftherias • Map N5 • 28420 26136

8 Mocca Cafe & Lounge Bar, Agios Nikolaos

Ices, crepes and cocktails are on offer at this popular beachside café. ◈ Kitroplatia Beach • Map N4 • 28410 24409

9 Amnesia, Kato Zakros

The place to go after dark if you are looking for more than a quiet brandy, if only for the fact that this is the resort's sole gesture towards an upbeat nightlife. ◈ Seafront • Map R5

10 Café Olympio, Makrygialos

Overlooking the small harbour, this relaxing café-bar offers full breakfasts, salads, tasty snacks, draught beer and cocktails. ◈ Makrygialos Harbour • Map P5 • 28430 52135

Café Olympio, Makrygialos

For more restaurants, tavernas, bars, cafés and ouzeries See pp68–73

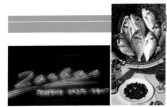

Price Categories

For a three-course	€	under €12
meal for one with half	€€	€12–€18
a bottle of wine (or	€€€	€18–€24
equivalent meal), taxes	€€€€	€24–€32
and extra charges.	€€€€€	over €32

Left **Zorbas, Siteia** Right **Fish from Zakros**

🔟 Places to Eat

1 The Old Mill, Elounda
The most luxurious restaurant in eastern Crete is situated in the Elounda Mare Hotel (see p126). The menu combines the best of Greece with international cuisine. Booking essential; formal dress code. ◎ Elounda Mare Hotel • Map N4 • 28410 68200 • Closed Nov–Mar • €€€€€

2 Balcony, Siteia
Located on the first floor of an elegant townhouse, Balcony serves Greek food with Asian and Mexican influences. It has an impressive wine list with plenty of local options. ◎ Foundalidou 19 • Map Q4 • 28430 25084 • €€€€€

3 Zorbas, Siteia
This long-established taverna serves freshly grilled fish and lobster, Cretan dishes, charcoal-grilled meats and meze. ◎ Harbourfront • Map Q4 • 28430 22689 • €€

4 Akrogiali, Kato Zakros
A relaxed spot on the beach, Akrogiali serves drinks, tasty seafood and grilled meat. ◎ On the beach • Map R5 • 28430 26893 • €€€

5 Kalliotzina, Koutsouras
This friendly taverna offers home-cooked meals, set at outside tables overhung by tamarisk trees. ◎ Seafront • Map P5 • 28430 51207 • Closed Nov–Apr • €€

6 Pelagos, Agios Nikolaos
A fine old taverna close to the fishing harbour, noted locally for its seafood. Its courtyard suits summer dining. ◎ Korakaiand Katehaki • Map N4 • 28410 25737 • Closed Nov–Mar • €€€€

7 Poulis, Elounda
Catering mainly for visitors, the menu here has Greek and international dishes, a long list of grilled seafood and a reasonable wine list. ◎ Harbourfront • Map N4 • 28410 41451 • Closed Nov–Apr • €€€

8 Stratos Restaurant, Makrygialos
Delicious fish meals are served here along with traditional Cretan favourites. ◎ Kalamokanias Beach • Map P5 • 28430 52357 • €€€

9 Taverna Ta Kochilia, Mochlos
With fantastic views of St Nikolaos Island, this traditional taverna offers Greek dishes and excellent seafood specialities. ◎ Mochlos Village • Map P4 • 28430 94432 • €€€

10 Gorgona, Ierapetra
Located on the seafront between the harbour and the fort, Gorgona is popular with visitors and locals alike. It serves classic Cretan dishes and good fish and seafood. ◎ Stratigou Samouil 12 • Map N6 • 28420 26619 • €€€

Akrogiali, Kato Zakros

STREETSMART

CRETE'S TOP 10

Left **Long-distance ferry** Centre **Local bus** Right **Vehicles for hire**

Getting To and Around Crete

1 Scheduled Flights

From Easter to late-October, a wide range of airlines serve Crete. Low-cost flights, such as easyJet, Ryanair and Jet, fly in from several airports in the UK. Olympic Airlines and Aegean Airlines connect Crete with other Greek destinations. In winter, travel to Crete via Athens. The website: www.travel.creteforyou.com/flights.html provides comprehensive information in this regard.

2 Charter Flights

Charter airlines owned by large package holiday companies fly to Chania and Irakleio from most airports in the UK and large mainland EU cities in summer. The first departures are usually around Easter, with the last return flight in late October. Most flights are sold as a package with accommo-dation and car rental.

3 Ferries

Fast ferries sail overnight, every night, between Piraeus, the port of Athens, and Irakleio on Crete. There are also (less frequent) ser-vices to Chania. Another popular option is to island-hop, staying for a few nights on one or more of the Cyclades.

4 Car Hire

There are local and international car rental companies at every airport, resort and major town in Crete. Renting on the spot is often more expensive than booking in advance with a major firm. Drive defensively and cautiously at all times – Greece has one of the worst accident rates in Europe.

5 Buses

Local buses operated by the KTEL consortium are a cheap and cheerful way to see Crete and meet local people. Tickets are cheap and there are regular departures even to remote villages. English-language timetables are usually available from local tourist offices.

6 Taxis

Taxis are surprisingly affordable, and operate not only in towns but on long journeys between towns and villages. Short journeys are metered, but for longer trips there is usually a fixed price – agree it before setting off. Most drivers speak some English, and vehi-cles are usually modern Mercedes saloons.

7 Local Boats

The only way to travel between Sougia and Chora Sfakion on the south coast is by boat. In summer, small boats putter along at least once a day, calling at Agia Roumeli and Loutro.

8 Riding

Mule or pony trekking is a great way to explore the awesome mountain scenery of the Lefka Ori (White Mountains), where there are still few motor roads.

9 Bicycle

Away from the north coast and its busy high-way, there are hundreds of miles of farm tracks and jeep roads which are ideal mountain-biking territory. Cycling is best enjoyed in spring (April–May) and autumn (late September–October).

10 Motorbikes and Scooters

Two-wheeled transport is popular with summer visitors. However, great caution should be used, both on busy roads and off-track. Helmets are compulsory and should be worn at all times *(see also p118)*.

Directory

Airports
Chania
28210 83800
• Irakleio
28103 97800

Airlines
Aegean Air 21062 61000, http://en.aegean air.com • Olympic 21035 50500, www.olympicair.com

Ferries
www.ferries.gr

Buses
bus-service-crete.com

Left **Local tourist information centre** Centre **Sign about etiquette** Right **Locked church**

🔟 General Information

When To Go
December, January and February are cold and wet, with snow on the mountains. Spring flowers begin to appear in March, but sunbathing is not a real option until April, and rain is possible until May. Temperatures start to climb seriously in June, peaking at 35°C or higher in July. October can be beautiful, with sunny days and cool nights, and even November can be a good month for sightseeing, though not for the beach. Most accommodation closes between Nov–Mar.

Passports and Visas
UK visitors require a passport; most other EU nationals require only a valid identity card. Citizens of the USA, Canada, Australia and New Zealand do not require visas for a stay of up to 90 days.

Customs
Visitors from other EU countries are not subject to customs formalities. Unauthorized export of antiquities and works of art is a serious offence. If bringing prescription drugs with you, also bring a copy of the prescription and, if possible, a letter from your doctor to say why you need them.

Tourist Offices Abroad
The Greek National Tourism Organisation, also known as the Hellenic Tourist Organisation and referred to by its Greek acronym, EOT, has closed most of its overseas offices due to financial cuts. For more information, check: www.visitgreece.gr.

Tourist Offices in Crete
EOT has offices in Irakleio, Chania and Rethymno. There are also local tourist offices in the major resorts. All have English-speaking staff who can provide maps, bus timetables, and lists of places to stay and things to see. Most will also help you to find accommodation.

Opening Hours
Opening hours on Crete are erratic. Use the times given in this book as a rough guide only. Most state-run museums and archaeological sites are open from around 8am–8pm, and most close on Mondays. However, timings may vary, so call to check in advance. Monasteries, convents and churches are generally open during daylight hours but close for two to three hours in the afternoon. Some smaller churches may be locked; the key is usually held in the nearest village shop or *kafeneion*.

Etiquette
Speaking even a few words of the language often works wonders in establishing a rapport with Cretans. Modest clothing (long trousers for men, over-the-knee skirts for women) is required when visiting monasteries and churches. Topless sunbathing is generally tolerated, but nude bathing is restricted to designated beaches.

Electricity
Greece uses the standard European 220V/50Hz AC electrical supply. Plugs have two round pins.

Clothing
A sun-hat and sunglasses are essential. In spring and autumn, a light wool sweater or fleece and a light windproof and waterproof jacket are useful. Good walking boots are a must for serious hiking.

Useful Accessories
A small torch is good in places with little street lighting. Take at least a litre of water if you plan even an easy walk. Mosquito repellents are supplied in most guesthouses. A snorkel and mask, and compact binoculars are handy if you want to observe wildlife.

Directory
Tourist Police
171

GNTO
www.visitgreece.gr
• See also p12, p18 & p22

Left **Sea urchins** Centre **Motorbikes and scooters** Right **Sun without shade**

Things to Avoid

1 Sunburn
Never underestimate the burning power of the Cretan sun, which can be punishing as early as April. Use a high-factor sunscreen or sunblock, especially on boat trips, when the sea breeze can make it seem deceptively cool, and take to the shade from midday until late afternoon.

2 Heatstroke
Heatstroke is another risk in high summer. Do not attempt strenuous hiking or mountain riding in July or August, drink plenty of water and wear a hat. Symptoms can be aggravated by alcohol – drink an extra half litre of water for each unit of alcohol you consume.

3 Mosquitoes
A night-time pest in many parts of Crete, mosquitoes breed in ponds, streams and cisterns. Out of doors, they can be kept away by deterrents containing diethyltoluamide ("deet") or the organic citronella oil. Indoors, use an electrical deterrent pad, sold in shops all over Crete.

4 Sea Urchins
Spiky black sea urchins infest most rocky beaches and can inflict a painful wound if stepped on in bare feet. Watch where you walk in shallow water. The spines, which snap off in the wound, can be pulled out with tweezers.

5 Jellyfish
Jellyfish, called *tsouchtres* in Greek, occasionally infest Cretan beaches. Most are harmless but some can inflict a painful sting. Rinsing with vinegar or a mild ammonia solution is an effective remedy, and an anti-histamine tablet and cream will also reduce inflammation.

6 Snakes
Crete has numerous snakes, most of which are completely harmless and none of which have a lethal bite (though the adder, rarely seen sunbathing on sunny rocks in the mountains, has a venomous bite). Most Greek villagers will kill any snake, venomous or not, on sight, and all Cretan snakes will flee when humans approach.

7 Renting a Motorbike
Many visitors with no previous experience of riding a motorbike or scooter rent a cheap and cheerful two-wheeler, and each year brings its crop of accidents. Riding in Crete is risky, even for experienced bikers. The inexperienced should stick to four wheels. If you must rent a bike, wear a helmet at all times. Wear long trousers and a jacket, which give you a bit more protection than shorts and T-shirt if you do take a tumble.

8 Kamakis
The native male *kamaki* ("harpooner") is a summer phenomenon. These amateur gigolos are convinced that female visitors are intent on an authentic Greek holiday romance, and are more than happy to supply it. Most will take a firm "no" for an answer.

9 Hornets
These large, red and black cousins of the wasp inflict a very painful sting and should not be handled or provoked. They are often seen hovering around pools of water or drinking fountains, but will not attack if left alone.

10 Photographing Military Installations
Greek authorities are extremely sensitive on issues of national security, as a group of British plane-spotters discovered in 2002, when they were arrested and convicted of espionage after taking photographs of Greek Air Force warplanes. Do not take photographs of military airfields (which often adjoin civil airports), army bases or radar installations (which are dotted around Crete's coasts and mountains), or naval vessels (even in civil harbours), or you are likely to be charged with spying. Prohibited sites are signposted with the symbol of a camera barred by a red stripe.

Left **Cycling** Centre **Windsurfing** Right **Cruise ship**

🔟 Special Interest Holidays

Archaeology

The ancient palace sites and ruined cities of Minoan and Hellenistic Crete can be confusing without a guide. Escorted tours featuring in-depth exploration of Knosos and other sites, with guest experts and slide shows, are offered by several companies.

Wildlife and Ornithology

The best times to seek out Crete's people-shy animals are spring and autumn, when specialist eco-tourism operators offer wildlife and walking holidays in many areas of Crete.

Walking and Hiking

Crete's highest mountains offer some of Europe's most inspiring wilderness walking, but can be lethal to inexperienced or lone walkers. Small group treks led by experienced guides can be safer.

Riding

Some companies, such as EcoGreece, offer horseback- or mule-riding expeditions through the Cretan countryside and into the Lefka Ori.

Cycling

A number of specialist companies offer accompanied cycling holidays in Crete, usually in spring and autumn, when it's not too hot for comfort, with most of your luggage travelling ahead of you by minibus each day and back-up transport available if the going gets too tough.

Painting

Spring is the most popular time for painting holidays in Crete, when the clear light and multi-coloured blaze of wild flowers provide inspirational subject matter. Some painting holidays can be combined with tours of archaeological sites and wildlife areas.

Music and Dance

Cretans are proud of their rich heritage of traditional music and dance, and eager to share it with visitors. A growing number of holidays, usually with accommodation in village homes, enable you to learn some of the complicated dances.

Windsurfing

The strong summer breezes which spring up most afternoons make Cretan coasts ideal for windsurfing. Most major tour operators offer packages with windsurfing coaching at major resorts such as Georgioupoli and Chersonisos.

Diving

Scuba diving is another burgeoning pastime in Crete. Many wrecks lie in shallow waters not far offshore, and visibility is excellent. Most ancient shipwrecks are off-limits to divers, but there are plenty of wartime wrecks to explore.

Cruising and Island-Hopping

Cruise vessels from a number of major cruise lines call at Cretan ports including Chania and Rethymno as part of itineraries which also include ports of call on the mainland and other islands. Multi-centre island-hopping holidays including a stay in Crete are also offered by some specialist companies.

Specialist Tours

Diktynna Travel
Archontaki 6, Chania
• *28210 41458 (escorted tours of museums, ancient sites and areas of natural beauty)* • *www. diktynna-travel.gr*

Walking Holidays
Kastellos, Rethymno
• *69749 94598*
• *www.footscapesof-crete.com*

Olympic Bike Travel
Adelianos Kampos, Rethymno • *28310 72383* • *www.olympic bike.com*

EcoGreece
1-877 838 7748 (USA)
• *www.ecogreece.com*

Green Tour
28310 20476 (guided walks, botanical tours and holidays)
• *www.greentour.gr*

Left **Traditional café** Centre **Raki bottles** Right **Café-bar, Agios Nikolaos**

Eating and Drinking Tips

1 Traditional Cafés
The old-fashioned *kafeneion* is a hub of village and town life, where local men gather to play backgammon and talk politics. They usually serve only Greek coffee, *frappé* (iced coffee), *ouzo* and *raki*, Greek brandy, bottled beer and a limited range of soft drinks.

2 Ouzeris and Mezedopoleion
These are the Greek equivalent of the Spanish tapas bar, serving *ouzo*, wine, beer and a range of snacks (*meze*) to accompany your drink. In a *mezedopoleion* you can order a complete meal of a dozen tiny dishes.

3 Pastry Shops
The *zacharoplasteion* (patisserie) is evidence of the Greek love of all things sweet. You will find honey-soaked baclava and an array of pastries stuffed with raisins and nuts and powdered with sugar and cinnamon, cream-filled pies and chocolate gateaux. The *zacharoplasteion* also serves coffee and sometimes a range of liqueurs and spirits.

4 Fish Restaurants
The *psarotaverna* (fish tavern) serves every imaginable kind of seafood, from tiny whitebait to whole sea bass, shrimp, octopus, squid, langouste and less familiar delicacies, including sea urchins. Fish is officially classed category "A" (the most expensive) through "E" and is priced by weight.

5 Grill Restaurants
The *psitesteatoreon* or grill restaurant is a carnivore's delight and a vegetarian's nightmare. The typical menu comprises chicken, lamb and pork, spit-grilled and served with chips and salad. Less familiar dishes include *kokoretsi* (liver and other offal wrapped in intestines and grilled) and sheep's head.

6 Giros (Kebab) Stands
The ubiquitous *giros* (pronounced "hero") is Greece's own greasy and delicious fast food – slivers of veal, pressed into a vertical cylinder and cooked on a revolving grill, shaved off and served in flat pitta bread with onions, tomatoes, yoghurt and a dash of cayenne pepper. *Giros* stands are strategically located in most towns and larger villages.

7 Café-Bars
Neon-lit, gleaming café-bars cater to holiday crowds in main resorts and to younger Greeks in towns such as Irakleio, Chania and Rethymno. They serve expensive imported lagers, iced coffee, soft drinks and disturbingly powerful cocktails, usually based on locally made vodka, tequila, rum or gin.

8 Raki and Wine
Tsikoudia, or *raki*, is Crete's fiery traditional tipple, and is served neat in tiny glasses, sometimes first thing in the morning with coffee. Cretans rarely drink more than one at a sitting; nor should you. Wines include pine resin-flavoured *retsina* (sold straight from the barrel or in 500 ml bottles) and drinkable red and white wines from Crete and elsewhere in Greece (*see also p71*).

9 Beer
Lager beers including Amstel and Heineken are brewed under licence in Greece and sold in 500 ml bottles. Local brands including Mythos and Fix (the first beer brewed in Greece, introduced by a Bavarian brewer in the 1840s), also in 500 ml bottles. Café-bars also serve imported brands including Budweiser and Beck's. Bottled Newcastle Brown Ale, Guinness and British keg lagers on draft are served in some holiday resorts.

10 Water and Soft Drinks
Greek tap water is perfectly safe to drink, but many visitors and Greeks themselves prefer the taste of bottled mineral water. Virtually every resort shop has a fridge stuffed with mineral water, cola, lemonade and other soft drinks.

Left **Herbs and spices for sale** Centre **Olive oils** Right **Pottery souvenirs**

Shopping Tips

1 Shop Opening Times

Cretan markets are busiest and best early in the morning, opening at about 7:30am Monday to Saturday, and busiest of all on Saturday mornings. Markets, and all other shops, close around midday, reopening around 5pm and staying open until at least 8pm. In resort areas, many shops are open until around 11pm in summer.

2 Tax and Allowances

Non-EU residents can reclaim Value Added Tax (VAT) on most goods by presenting the relevant receipt at Customs on departure. Non-EU travellers can also buy wines, spirits, tobacco, perfumes and other goods in duty-free shops at Chania and Irakleio airports.

3 Prices and Bargaining

Bargaining over prices is not common practice in Crete, and most ticket prices are fairly fixed. That said, it never hurts to ask for the best possible price, especially in art and craft shops. Prices are often notably cheaper at the very end of the holiday season, when custom is on the wane.

4 Cash or Credit?

Most traders and shop owners (as well as restaurant and small hotel owners) prefer cash to credit cards, and usually pass on to you the percentage charged by the credit card company, which can be as much as 5 per cent.

5 Wine

Aided by modern wine-making techniques, Greek wines are coming into their own, and the vineyards of Crete are no exception. The Boutari wines are among the best, and you can buy quality wines to take home in most towns and at airports.

6 Herbs

Crete is famous for the healing and cleansing properties of its wild mountain herbs, which are gathered, dried and exported in bulk all over Greece. Take home a big bag of sage, oregano, thyme or basil, sold loose or in packages in the markets of Chania, Rethymno and Irakleio.

7 Olives and Olive Oil

Olives and olive oil have been staples of the Greek diet since ancient times, and the olive groves of Crete produce some of the best. Cold pressed virgin olive oil is the key ingredient of many dishes, and quality oil (you really can taste the difference) is much cheaper in Crete than at home.

8 Pottery

Pottery-making is a living skill on Crete: look out for prettily coloured, modern bowls, plates and cups, simple old-fashioned peasant earthenware, or copies of elaborately decorated Minoan, Classical or Hellenistic ceramics.

9 Carved Wood

Unique to Crete is the curly wooden stick carved from *prinos* wood, which is the mountain shepherd's versatile tool, used to carry burdens, discipline dogs and encourage stubborn mules. They make handsome wall decorations. You may also find attractive bowls and platters turned from hard, close-grained olive wood.

10 Icons, Antiques and Handicrafts

Original icons of saints, archangels and apostles command high prices and require an export licence – reputable dealers will assist in obtaining the necessary permissions. Good copies can be bought from specialist dealers, and from museum shops in Irakleio and Chania. Look out too for antique daggers, silver pen and tobacco cases, meerschaum pipes and flintlock pistols – but beware of fakes. Colourful woolen blankets and rugs are easy to carry home, as are beautifully embroidered textiles.

Left **Ferry** Centre **Camping sign** Right **Market food**

Budget Ideas

1 Off-Season Travel
The cost of living rockets from mid-June to early September. Accommodation, air fares to Crete, and car and scooter rental are lower in spring and autumn. The best time of all for a budget visit is early October, when the sea is warm and there is still plenty of sun but few visitors.

2 Cheap Flights and Ferries
A number of flights connect the UK and Europe to Crete, between the months of April and November. Low-cost airlines have opened several routes, so fares are competitive. In winter, it is requisite to fly to Crete via Athens. Ferries run daily from the port of Piraeus in Athens to Crete all year round.

3 Discounts
The longer you intend to stay in one place, the cheaper your room will be. Pensions and hotels usually offer a 10 per cent discount for three nights or more, and you may get an even better rate if staying for several weeks. Most museums and archaeological sites offer cheap admission for students and school pupils.

4 Youth Hostels
There are youth hostels in Irakleio, Chersonisos, Rethymno, Siteia and Plakias, with dormitory beds (for around one-third the cost of a cheap room) and basic kitchen facilities.

5 Camping
Camping can save you some money, with most campsites charging around half the cost of a budget room for a tent and two people. On the downside, few campsites are easy to get to using public transport, and camping means carrying a tent.

6 Working Holidays
Finding casual work picking fruit or olives is less easy than it was, as migrants from Albania and other eastern European countries provide a supply of cheap labour. Bar and restaurant work in resorts is very poorly paid (most earnings are from tips), with very long hours. If you have a degree in English, you may find work teaching in a private language school. In theory, EU citizens do not need work permits.

7 Hitch-hiking
Hitching can be a good way of getting around the island (especially to out-of-the-way spots), and Cretans themselves frequently hitch-hike. Off the beaten track, where there is little traffic, you may have to wait for hours in hot sun.

8 Cheap Eats
Giros stands *(see p120)* offer the cheapest tasty hot meals in Crete. Markets are piled with inexpensive fruit in summer, and if you stick to picnicking on fruit, olives, cheese and fresh-baked bread (the healthy diet of the Cretan villager), you can live on surprisingly little. In restaurants, Greek salad (onions, cucumber, tomatoes, olives and a slab of feta cheese, drowned in oil) is a cheap meal in its own right. Fish is always the most expensive dish on any menu, and chicken and squid are usually the cheapest.

9 Drinking and Entertainment
A half-litre bottle of beer or a half-litre of wine in an old-fashioned local café is usually half the price of a smaller beer or a fancy cocktail in a smart café-bar. Admission to most discos and clubs in resorts is free, but drinks are expensive. Make the most of half-price happy hour in lively resorts like Chersonisos and Malia.

10 Resorts to Avoid
Budget travellers should avoid the purpose-built north coast resorts – including Elounda, Malia, Chersonisos, Bali and Georgioupoli – which cater to a captive market of high-spending holidaymakers.

Left **Aqua park** Centre **Car hire** Right **Family on the beach**

🔟 Families and Disabled Visitors

1 Hotels
All hotels in Crete welcome children. Most major holiday companies now feature hotels which are especially family-friendly, with facilities such as babysitting and activity clubs. Larger hotels used by major European holiday companies often have some rooms specifically designed for wheelchair users and for people with other disabilities.

2 Self-Catering Apartments and Villas
Small self-catering complexes are a popular family choice. Villas with pools can be ideal for families. On the down side, most villas on Crete are some distance from the beach.

3 Activities for Children
Some package holiday hotels offer a range of supervised activities for younger children. Crete also has a couple of aquaparks, with wave pools and waterslides, close to main resorts. Older children can enjoy pedalos, sea canoes, and windsurfing at resorts.

4 Feeding Children
Children may find some Greek restaurant dishes (like fish with the head still attached) intimidating. Western-style dishes, such as spaghetti, hamburgers and chips are served in all resorts.

5 Baby Necessities
Familiar brands of baby milk, baby food and nappies for infants are available at mini-markets in the resorts, or the local *geniko emporion* (general store) or pharmacy.

6 Child Safety on the Beach
Children should wear sunblock and a hat on the beach as there is a risk of severe sunburn even as early as April. Warn children to look out for spiny black sea urchins. There are no lifeguards.

7 Cars and Buses
Rental cars are fitted with safety belts, but child seats may not be available. For short journeys, use taxis rather than slow and crowded local buses. There are no disabled facilities at bus stations, but collapsible wheelchairs may be carried in the luggage compartment of long-distance buses.

8 Wheelchair Access at Airports
The airports of both Chania and Irakleio have wheelchair access. Chania airport has wheelchair facilities and access throughout the airport, while Irakleio airport can make arrangements for wheelchair access to flights.

9 Wheelchair Access at Sights
Few visitor attractions or museums are fully accessible to wheelchair users, but some have ramps from street level and lifts to upper storeys. Most archaeological sites in Crete are located on steep and rugged land, with rough paths or steps and few, if any, ramps.

10 Organizations for Disabled Visitors
In the UK, several organizations, most easily found through www.disabilities-online.com/travel, and RADAR provide advice on travel and accommodation in Greece for people with disabilities. Disabled Holiday Directory lists holidays for the disabled.

Directory

Tourism for All
*7A Pixel Mill,
44 Appley Rd, Kendal,
Cumbria LA9 6ES, UK
• 0845 1249 971 • www.
tourismforall.org.uk*

RADAR
*12 City Forum, 250
City Rd, London EC1V
8AF • 020 7250 3222
• www.radar.org.uk*

Disabled Holiday Directory
*Premier House,
Manchester Rd,
Mossley OL5 9AA
• 0800 993 0796
• www.disabledholiday
directory.co.uk*

Left **Post boxes** Centre **Bank sign** Right **Telephone booth**

🔟 Banking and Communications

1 Language
English is spoken more or less fluently by virtually all Cretans working in hotels, guesthouses and other tourist-related industries, and in most bars and restaurants. However, learning a few words of Greek, even if only those for "hello" *(yiassou* or *kalimera),* "please" *(parakalo)* and "thank you" *(efkaristo),* will be much appreciated.

2 Changing Money
Like most EU member states, Greece adopted the euro in 2002. Change money or travellers' cheques at banks in larger towns and villages, at post offices displaying a yellow "Exchange" sign, and at travel agencies and some hotels in holiday resorts. Always take your passport when changing money. Banks are normally open 8am–2pm Monday to Thursday, 8am–1:30pm Friday.

3 Credit Cards
Credit cards are widely accepted in larger hotels, more expensive shops and in some tourist restaurants, but cash is preferred in most stores, guesthouses and tavernas. Some establishments charge an additional 4–5 per cent for credit card use. You can also use your credit or debit card to withdraw euros from ATMs in all larger towns and at airports.

4 Public Phones
Phones are plentiful and efficient, with separate booths for local and international calls. International booths are prominently marked, and there are multilingual instructions in all phone boxes. Most use a prepaid phone card, available from most general stores and street kiosks, and this is the cheapest way of calling home. You can also use metered phones in local offices of OTE, the Greek telecommunications organization.

5 Mobile Phones
European cellphone users should experience no problems in using their phones in Crete. However, coverage may be patchy in some mountain areas and in deep valleys such as the Samaria Gorge. Some US and Canadian mobile phones systems may not yet be fully compatible with Greek networks.

6 Post Offices
The post office *(taxidromeion)* is indicated by a round yellow sign and is usually open 7:30am–2pm Monday to Friday. Some post offices also exchange money and traveller's cheques.

7 Fax and Poste Restante
Faxes can be sent from OTE offices and from some travel agencies and hotels. Mail marked "Poste Restante" can be held for you at main post offices. Be aware that you will need proof of identity to collect your mail.

8 Internet
Internet cafés with cheap broadband access can be found in all main towns and resorts. Internet booking is the quickest and easiest way to book accommodation, excursions, rental cars, tours and transportation.

9 TV and Radio
The BBC World Service can be received on 9.41, 15.07 and 12.09 Mhz shortwave. Most hotels in C category (3-star) and above have satellite TV receiving Sky and CNN. Voice of America English-language broadcasts also come through clearly.

10 Newspapers
Most European newspapers can be bought in resorts the day after publication. The *International Herald Tribune,* published daily, carries worldwide news and US sports reports, and includes an English edition of the main Greek daily, *Kathimerini.* For news from North America, *USA Today* is on sale in many resorts. Also published in English is the daily *Athens News,* with Greek and international reports.

Left **Cretan policeman** Centre **Medical unit** Right **Pharmacy**

⁇10 Health and Security Tips

EOT/GNTO
The EOT/GNTO organization helps tourists who encounter problems with hotels, campsites, car rental and tour companies while in Crete.

Travel Insurance
You should take out comprehensive travel insurance covering you for private medical treatment and for evacuation if necessary, as well as for loss or theft of belongings and expenses incurred due to delayed or cancelled flights. Make sure your policy will pay for medical and hospital fees direct and that it covers you for holiday activities such as trekking, scuba diving, riding, and motorcycling, as well as for personal liability in the event of damage to rented cars or motorcycles.

Minor Ailments
Sunburn and heat exhaustion and mosquito bites are easily prevented (see p118). A basic medical kit should include painkillers, anti-histamine tablets and cream for bites and stings, a diarrhoea remedy, and motion sickness tablets for boat or bus journeys.

Insects and Pests
Hornets, scorpions and (possibly) vipers all exist in Crete but are not dangerous unless handled.

Their bites and stings are painful but not normally lethal to adults, though medical attention should be sought if small children are bitten.

Breakdowns and Accidents
Set up a warning triangle if possible – your hire car should be equipped with one. If anyone is injured, passers-by are required to stop and help, and you must contact the police. If involved in a collision, never admit liability, sign any statement of responsibility, or lose your temper. Contact your travel insurance company as soon as possible.

Doctors
There are private medical clinics in all the main towns. Many doctors speak good English. Consultations must be paid for in cash.

Dentists
Dentists are proficient and can be found in major towns including Irakleio, Chania, Rethymno, Agios Nikolaos, Siteia and Ierapetra. You must pay for your treatment in cash.

Hospitals
A European Health Insurance Card covers any necessary medical treatment for EU citizens in Greek public hospitals but it is much better to make sure your insurance covers private treatment.

Pharmacies
Greek pharmacists provide comprehensive advice on minor ailments and injuries, and can dispense a wide range of remedies including antibiotics, anti-inflammatories and painkillers. Most speak good English. Pharmacies (farmakia) are marked by a green cross sign.

Crime
Crete has a very low crime rate and is one of the safest holiday destinations in the world. However, thefts from tourists do occur. Take sensible precautions, including locking rental cars and hotel rooms, and keeping passports, tickets and spare cash in hotel safes.

Emergencies

Multilingual for all types of emergency
112
Police
100
Tourist Police
171
Ambulance
166
Fire
199
Forest fire
191
Roadside assistance
104 00
Coastguard
108
EOT/GNTO
Contact nearest tourist office

Left **Atlantica Caldera Creta Paradise** Right **Grecotel Creta Palace**

Luxury Resorts

1 Elounda Mare Hotel, Elounda
Undeniably the best resort hotel in Crete, the Elounda Mare is a complex of 215 rooms and villas set in lush grounds. It offers tennis and a full array of water sports. Other facilities are close by on the peninsula. ✆ Elounda Beach, 72053 • Map N4 • 28410 68200 • www.eloundamare.com • €€€€€

2 Hotel St Nicolas Bay, Agios Nikolaos
Within walking distance of the restaurants and shops of Agios Nikolaos, this fine hotel has three swimming pools and its own semi-private beach. ✆ 72100 Agios Nikolaos • Map N4 • 28410 90200 • www.stnicolasbay.gr • Closed Nov–Mar • €€€€€

3 Creta Maris Beach Resort, Chersonisos
Right on the beach, Creta Maris aims for a village atmosphere with paths winding through green grounds past a mix of bungalows, suites and rooms. It also offers a luxurious spa and activities such as Cretan dancing and cooking courses. ✆ Limin Chersonisos • Map L4 • 28970 27000 • www.maris.gr/creta • €€€€€

4 Elounda Peninsula, Elounda
On its own private peninsula, this hotel has duplex suites as well as larger villas with private pools. Facilities include a spa, tennis courts and a kids' club. ✆ South of Elounda • Map N4 • 28410 68250 • www.elounda peninsula.com • €€€€€

5 Minoa Palace Resort & Spa, Platanias
Close to both Platanias and Chania, Minoa Palace has a variety of rooms, suites and bungalows, some with their own private pools. ✆ Agias Marinas • Map C2 • 28210 36500 • www.minoapalace.gr • €€€€€

6 Blue Palace Resort and Spa, Elounda
Superb mix of luxury suites, bungalows and villas with spa, health centre, indoor and outdoor pools and tennis courts, plus a range of water sports. ✆ Plakas Elounda 72100 • Map N4 • 28410 65500 • www.bluepalace.gr • Closed Nov–Mar • €€€€€

7 Atlantica Caldera Creta Paradise, Chania
An award-winning 186-room resort on one of Crete's Blue Flag beaches, the Creta Paradise is only ten minutes away from the centre of Chania. Facilities include two pools and a wellness spa. Its bungalows have been built in an attractive Neo-Classical style. ✆ 73100 Gerani • Map D2 • 28210 61315 • www.atlanticahotels.com • Closed Nov–Mar • €€€€€

8 Out of the Blue Capsis Elite Resort, Agia Pelagia, Irakleio
On a private headland, this five-star resort has its own private beaches, a huge pool, a choice of bars and restaurants and a children's club. Ideal for families, with some exclusive villas. ✆ Agia Pelagia 75100, Irakleio • Map K3 • 28108 11112 • www.capsis.com • Closed Nov–Mar • €€€€€

9 Grecotel Creta Palace, Rethymno
The Creta Palace is only 4 km (2 miles) from central Rethymno, with 162 rooms in its main block and 200 bungalows and villas. It has several pools and a wide range of activities for children, as well as tennis and water sports. ✆ 74100 Missiria • Map F3 • 28310 55181 • www.grecotel.com • Closed Nov–Mar • €€€€€

10 Minos Beach Art Hotel, Agios Nikolaos
This medium-sized complex of bungalows with splendid views of the Gulf of Mirabello is set in tranquil, flower-filled gardens. Only a stroll from the centre of Agios Nikolaos, the hotel has its own sandy beaches and rocky inlets. ✆ 72100 Ag • Map N4 • 28410 22345 • www.minosbeach.com • Closed Nov–Mar • €€€€€

Note: Unless otherwise stated, all hotels accept credit cards, have en suite bathrooms and air conditioning

Price Categories

For a standard, double room per night (with breakfast if included), taxes and extra charges.

€	under €30
€€	€30–€40
€€€	€40–€80
€€€€	€80–€120
€€€€€	over €120

Left **Mythos Suites** Right **Palazzo Rimondi**

🔟 Boutique Hotels

1 Mythos Suites, Rethymno

Situated in the old part of Rethymno, this smart hotel is housed in two 16th-century Venetian buildings that have been knocked into one. They surround a courtyard with a pretty pool; ground-floor rooms have verandahs adjoining the courtyard, while upper-floor rooms have wooden balconies. ◈ C12 Plateia Karaoli, 74100 • Map F3 • 28310 53917 • www.mythos-crete.gr • €€€€€

2 Palazzino di Corina, Rethymno

This lovingly restored Venetian mansion, right in the heart of the old town, has 29 luxury suites, some with Jacuzzi baths and four-poster beds. There's a tiny pool in the charming patio, a lively street-side bar and an excellent restaurant. ◈ Dambergi 7–9 • Map Q1 • 28310 21205/06 • www.corina.gr • €€€€

3 Palazzo Rimondi, Rethymno

Tucked away in an arcaded courtyard behind iron gates, Palazzo Rimondi is a well-restored complex of 15th-century buildings, with vaulted roofs, carved stone and wooden panelled ceilings. ◈ 21 Xanthoudidou and 16 Har. Trikoupi, 74100 • Map F3 • 28310 51001 • www.hotelsrimondi. com • Closed Nov–Mar • €€€€

4 Casa Delfino, Chania

This 17th-century Venetian mansion, Chania's most exclusive address, has been luxuriously restored. In a quiet alley, it has fine rooftop views and the suites have been individually designed. ◈ Theofanous 9, 73100 • Map D2 • 28210 93098 • www.casadelfino. com • €€€€€

5 Casa Leone, Chania

The "House of the Lion" has been meticulously restored, with period details such as Venetian mirrors and antique (and reproduction) furniture. The Casa Leone also has a smart cocktail bar. ◈ Parodos Theotokopolou 18 • Map D2 • 28210 76762 • www.casa-leone.com • €€€€€

6 Alcanea Boutique Hotel, Chania

Located in the harbour above the Naval Museum, this hotel occupies a historic building – once the office of Cretan revolutionary hero Eleftherios Venizelos. Rooms are simple and traditionally furnished with stunning views of the harbour and the sea. ◈ Angelou 2 • Map A5 • 28210 75370 • www.alcanea.com • Closed in winter • €€€€€

7 Lato Boutique Hotel, Irakleio

Open all year round, the Lato offers panoramic views of the Venetian Fortress and Irakleio's old port from its modern, comfortable rooms. ◈ 15 Epimenidou St, 71202 • Map T1 • 28102 28103 • www.lato.gr • €€€€

8 Kapsaliana Village Hotel, Arkadi

In this village, 12 houses of Cretan and Venetian architecture have been converted into 17 guesthouses, each combining original features with modern comforts such as Wi-Fi and DVD players. The complex has a pool, a restaurant and a tiny museum. ◈ Kapsaliana, near Arkadi • Map G4 • 28310 83400 • www. kapsalianavillage.gr • €€€€€

9 Villa Andromeda, Chania

A lovingly restored Neo-Classical mansion, with a lush palm garden and a large pool, elaborately painted ceilings, white marble floors, staircases and balconies. ◈ 150 Eleftherios Venizelou, 73133 • Map D2 • 28210 28300 • www.villandromeda.gr • Closed Nov–Mar • €€€€€

10 Suites Pandora, Chania

This is a stylish collection of two- and four-bed suites, some facing an inner courtyard, others looking out to sea. All have high ceilings, balconies and tall shuttered windows. ◈ Lithinon 29, 73100 • Map D2 • 28210 43588 • www.pandora-hotel.com • €€€€

Left **Casa Veneta** Centre **Natalia's Houses** Right **Anna Apartments, Paleochora**

TOP 10 Self-Catering Apartments

1 Elounda Residence, Elounda

Set in lush gardens about 20 minutes' walk from the village, this complex has 24-hour reception, bars, restaurant and mini-market to complement its two- to four-bed apartments. Facilities include a large saltwater pool, children's pool, tennis court and mini-golf. ✪ *72053 Elounda • Map N4 • 28410 41823 • www.eloundaresidence.gr • Closed Nov–Mar • €€€*

2 Casa Veneta, Chania

This Venetian mansion near the harbour has been divided into double and twin-bedded studios, and open-plan apartments sleeping up to four people, some with sea views. ✪ *Theotokopoulou 55–7, 73131 Chania • Map D2 • 28210 90007 • www.casaveneta.gr • Closed Nov–Mar • €€€*

3 Aptera Lodge, Aptera

These modern and well-equipped studio apartments near the ancient city of Aptera offer lovely views over Souda Bay and the White Mountains. ✪ *Aptera, Apokoronou, 73003 Chania • Map D2 • 28250 31440 • No credit cards • www.aptera-lodge.com • €€€*

4 Metohi Vai Village, Vai Beach

The only accommodation this close to the palm beach at Vai, the seven apartments at Metohi Vai occupy old shepherds' shelters, which have been converted to comfortable apartments with kitchens, satellite TVs and working fireplaces. ✪ *South of Vai Beach • Map R4 • 28430 22032 • www.palaikastro.com/metohivai • €€€*

5 Paul-Eva Apartments, Chersonisos

These very affordable apartments, only 1 km from the beach, come with private balconies and all the amenities you would expect, plus a shared pool. ✪ *70007 Chersonisos • Map M4 • 28970 23358 • Closed Nov–Mar • €€*

6 Stella's Traditional Apartments, Kato Zakros

Stella's has stone-built, traditionally furnished apartments set in flower gardens with seating areas and hammocks. All necessary comforts are included, from terraces and fully-equipped kitchens to fresh springwater on tap. ✪ *Kato Zakros village • Map R5 • 28430 23739 • www.stelapts.com • €€€*

7 Bay View Apartments, Siteia

On the fringe of Siteia and just a few paces from the beach, the Bay View has 10 apartments, most with twin beds and sofa-bed, and all with full kitchen facilities. Each room has a balcony or verandah. ✪ *Petras, 72300 • Map Q4 • 28430 24333 • No credit cards • No air conditioning • www.bayview-apartments.gr • Closed Nov–Mar • €€€*

8 Anna Apartments, Mirthios

Constructed in wood and stone, these family-run apartments have spectacular views of the Plakias Bay. Beautifully furnished, they come with a kitchenette, satellite TV and Wi-Fi. ✪ *Mirthios village • Map F4 • 697 3324 775 • www.annaview.com • €€€*

9 Natalia's Houses, Douliana

Each of these traditional apartments has a bathroom, balcony and a fully equipped kitchen. There is also a small shop, a pool, a bar and a barbecue area for guests' use. ✪ *Douliana village • Map E3 • 28250 23356 • www.nataliashouses.gr • €€€€*

10 Anna Apartments, Paleochora

Smothered with flowers and greenery, this little complex is on a quiet side street close to the beach. All apartments have a living room, kitchen, verandah and one or two bedrooms. There's also a children's play area. ✪ *Paleochora • Map B4 • 28103 46428 • No credit cards • www.villaanna-paleochora.com • €€€*

Note: Unless otherwise stated, all hotels accept credit cards, have en suite bathrooms and air conditioning

Price Categories

For a standard, double room per night (with breakfast if included), taxes and extra charges.

€	under €30
€€	€30–€40
€€€	€40–€80
€€€€	€80–€120
€€€€€	over €120

Left **Kalives Beach Hotel** Right **Porto Loutro Hotel**

TOP 10 Beach Hotels

1 Iberostar Creta Panorama & Mare, Rethymno

Four outdoor pools, a heated indoor pool, six tennis courts, sauna and water sports that include scuba diving make this huge beach resort one of the best in Crete for an active holiday. Accommodation is in suites or bungalows. ✆ *Panormo* • *Map F3* • *28340 51502* • *Closed Nov–Mar* • *www. iberostar.com* • *€€€€€*

2 Kalives Beach Hotel, Kalives

Situated between two sandy beaches on Souda Bay, this hotel overlooks the river and has 150 rooms in two wings, each with a pool. There is an attractive riverside terrace restaurant and easy beach access. ✆ *7303 Kalives* • *Map E2* • *28250 31285* • *www.kalyvesbeach.com* • *Closed Nov–Mar* • *€€€€*

3 Irini Mare, Agia Galini

Close to the sea and the village of Agia Galini, Irini Mare is a small, family-run hotel in a tranquil spot. There is a pool and a kids' playground too, and almost all the rooms have balconies with a sea view. Great buffet breakfast. ✆ *Main beach* • *Map G5* • *28320 91051* • *www. irinimare.com* • *€€€€€*

4 Porto Loutro Hotel, Loutro

This very attractive hotel just above the beach at Loutro has 36 rooms (plus four self-catering studios). They are in two buildings in separate parts of this village, set among palm trees, bougainvillea and tamarisk. It is accessible only by boat. ✆ *73011 Loutro, Anopoli* • *Map D4* • *28250 91433* • *No credit cards* • *www. hotelportoloutro.com* • *Closed Nov–Feb* • *€€€*

5 Istron Bay Hotel, Istro

Set in a peaceful location above a lovely cove, Istron Bay has several luxury suites, a lively beach bar and its own private beach. ✆ *Istro Bay, near Istro village* • *Map N5* • *28410 61303* • *www. istronbay.gr* • *€€€€€*

6 Astir Beach Hotel, Gouves

This hotel overlooks a fine, sandy beach and has two pools, a tennis court and a range of other land and water sports, including a scuba diving centre. It also has a children's playground. ✆ *70014 Gouves* • *Map L3* • *28970 41141* • *www. astirbeach.gr* • *Closed Nov–Mar* • *€€€€€*

7 Pilot Beach Resort, Georgioupolis

Georgioupolis's flagship resort has extensive sports facilities, pools, lots of fun activities for kids and well-appointed bungalows and suites. Enjoy Cretan food and nightlife in one of the resort's four restaurants and three bars. ✆ *East of Georgioupolis* • *Map E3* • *28250 61002* • *www. pilot-beach.gr* • *€€€€€*

8 Alianthos Garden Hotel, Plakias

Across the road from one of Crete's best beaches, this family-run hotel is the best in Plakias. It has a children's pool, freshwater pool and pool-bar, a supermarket and restaurant. ✆ *74060 Plakias* • *Map F4* • *28320 31280* • *www.alianthos.gr* • *Closed Dec–Feb* • *€€€€*

9 Grecotel Club Marine Palace, Panormos

Designed to look like a village, this modern family resort is set above a beautiful private cove and has several pools, two pool bars, a beach bar and organized activities. ✆ *Panormos village* • *Map G3* • *28340 51610* • *www.grecotel.com* • *€€€€€*

10 Sitia Bay Hotel, Siteia

This hotel has 19 rooms and apartments with kitchens and balconies with sea views. Amenities include satellite TV, free Wi-Fi and a rooftop terrace. There is also a small gym and a chlorine-free pool equipped with hydromassage. ✆ *Patriarhou Vartholomeou 27/Tritis Septemvriou 8* • *Map Q4* • *28430 24800* • *www.sitia-bay.com* • *€€€€€*

Left **Milia Village** Centre **Eleonas Traditional Resort** Right **The Blue House**

Village Guesthouses

1 Milia Village
Set in the forested slopes of Crete's "wild west", Milia offers 13 rooms in village houses rebuilt between 1982 and 1993 in local stone and wood. The rooms are heated by wood-burning stoves, while water comes from mountain springs. ◎ *73012 Milia, Vlatos • Map B3 • 28210 46774 • No air conditioning • www.milia.gr • €€€*

2 Rooms Aravanes, Thronos
The warm welcome, delicious home-grown food and, above all, the unsurpassable views of the Amari Valley and Mount Idi more than make up for the simple and basic rooms at this guesthouse. The owner, Lambros, is a mine of information and organizes hiking tours of the local area. ◎ *Thronos village • Map G4 • 28330 22760 • €€€*

3 Hotel Marina, Anogia
Beautifully situated in the picturesque village of Anogia, this modern three-star hotel offers a panoramic view of the Cretan landscape. The hotel has 16 apartments, including four larger ones for families. Each has a kitchen, TV, balcony with a view of the Psiloritis range and a fireplace for the winter months. ◎ *Main street • Map H4 • 28340 31817 • www.marinahotel anogia.gr • €€€*

4 Aspros Potamos Cottages, Makrygialos
This group of shepherds' cottages with stone floors, low wooden ceilings and corner fireplace nooks stands in groves of pine, olive and carob trees. The sandy beach at Makrygialos is less than 2 km (1 mile) away, and there is a tiny swimming pool on site. ◎ *Aspros Potamos, Makrygialos 72055, Ierapetra • Map P5 • 28430 51694 • No air conditioning • www.asprospotamos.com • €€€*

5 Terramara, Plakalon
Located on a hill surrounded by olive groves and mountains, Terramara offers spectacular views of the Gulf of Kisamos. The hotel is wonderful for a peaceful getaway. Facilities include a barbecue area, a pool and bar, and a laundry service. ◎ *Plakalon • Map B2 • 69406 94904 • No credit cards • www.terramara crete.com • €€€*

6 Arolithos, Tylissos
A complex of stone houses with an array of traditional crafts, from pottery and icon painting to basket weaving and embroidery. Traditional music and dance performed nightly. ◎ *Arolithos, 71500 Servili, Tylissos • Map J4 • 28108 21050 • www. arolithos.com • €€€*

7 Eleonas Cottages, Zaros
These 20 traditionally built cottages, scattered across the hillside, have galleried bedrooms. Facilities include kitchen, TV and fireplace. There's an excellent taverna that uses local produce. ◎ *Map H5 • 28940 31238 • www.eleonas.gr • €€€€*

8 The Blue House, Loutro
Amiable guest house, with balconies overlooking the bay and the slopes of the White Mountains. Particularly handy as an overnight stop on the way to or from Agia Roumeli and the Samaria Gorge. ◎ *Loutro • Map D4 • 28250 91127 • €€€*

9 Corali Studios and Portobello Apartments, Elounda
A short walk from the town centre, these studios and apartments offer good value for money. With their own pool and gardens, they serve as an ideal holiday home. ◎ *Akti Posidonos • Map N4 • 28410 41712 • www.coralistudios.com • €€€*

10 Koutsounari Cottages, Ierapetra
Hillside holiday village, with a choice of restored stone cottages with modern kitchens and bathrooms, or fully up-to-date studios. All have verandahs or tiny gardens, and there is a pool, snack bar and taverna next door. Minimum stay one week. ◎ *72200 Ierapetra • Map N6 • 28420 61815 • Some air conditioning • www.nakoutradition.gr • €€€€*

Note: Unless otherwise stated, all hotels accept credit cards, have en-suite bathrooms and air conditioning

Price Categories

For a standard, double room per night (with breakfast if included), taxes and extra charges.

€ under €30
€€ €30–€40
€€€ €40–€80
€€€€ €80–€120
€€€€€ over €120

Left **Villa Stratos** Right **Metohi Kindelis**

🔟 Villas

1 Elounda Gulf Villas

Crete's most luxurious villa complex has 18 villas and 10 suites, each with private pool. All have washing machines and dishwashers, and marble bathrooms with whirlpool tubs. Fine sea views are to be had; on fine days right across the Gulf of Mirabello. 🧭 72053 Elounda • Map N4 • 28102 27721 • www. eloundavillas.com • Closed Nov–Mar • €€€€€

2 Villa Stephanos, Rethymno

This villa is set in a private garden, in the village of Agios Dimitrios. With lovely views of the surrounding countryside, it is the perfect place to escape the hustle and bustle of city life. Well-equipped, it has a pool, and a daily maid service available on request. 🧭 Agios Dimitrios, Pigi • Map G3 • 28310 27597 • www.helidoniavillas-crete.gr • €€€€€

3 Villa Katikia-Gonia, Rethymno

Superbly furnished and well equipped, Villa Gonia is an exclusive holiday spot in Crete. Its terraces allow guests to enjoy scenic views of the countryside. There is a swimming pool and a pleasant garden too. The living room has an open fire for cool winter evenings. 🧭 Gonia, Rethymno • Map F3 • 28310 31282 • No credit cards • www.villa-gonia.gr • €€€€€

4 Villa Christina, Almirida

On a hilltop above Almirida beach, with a superb pool and views over Souda Bay. A double room, two twins, fully equipped kitchen and maid service. Also with a wonderful sea-facing terrace. 🧭 Plaka, Almirida • Map D2 • Reservations 69457 85673 • www.holidaylettings.co.uk • Closed Nov–Mar • €€€€€

5 Footscapes of Crete, Rethymno

There are wonderful views of the sea and mountains from these modern villas in the quiet village of Kastellos. Guided country walks are offered. 🧭 Kastellos, Rethymno • Map F3 • 69749 94598 • www.footscapesofcrete.com • €€€

6 Villa Therisso, Therisso

Far from the tourist mainstream, in the historic village of Therisso near Chania, this two-bedroom hillside villa is spacious and comfortable, with a pool, patios and fine views over Therisso Gorge. It offers a taste of traditional village life. 🧭 Therisso village • Map C3 • www.gicthevillacollection.com • (00 44) 75 4010 9935 • €€€€

7 Vamos Houses, Vamos

These are luxurious villas in a village of restored traditional buildings, with private courtyards and balconies. 🧭 Vamos • Map E3 • 28250 22190 • www.vamossa.gr • €€€€

8 Villa Stratos, Kalonyktis

A three-villa complex surrounded by flower- and fruit-filled gardens. The villas vary in size and two have their own pools. The pretty village of Kalonyktis, with its mini-market and taverna, is a short walk away. 🧭 Kalonyktis • Booking through Stratos Villas 28310 26956 • www.stratosvillas.com • €€€€€

9 Metohi Kindelis, Chania

Two villa apartments, each with its own garden and pool, within a huge family farmhouse dating from Venetian times. It is surrounded by apricot and orange groves, and a huge lawn. Inside, are cool marble floors and modern facilities. 🧭 Pervolia, Chania • Map D2 • 28210 41321 • No air conditioning • No credit cards • www.metohi-kindelis.gr • €€€€€

10 Zeus's House, Lasithi

Located in the heart of the lush Lasithi Plateau, this is a spacious, traditional two-bedroom house with many antique furnishings. There's a big garden with a pool, and plenty of trees for shade. 🧭 Agios Konstantinos village • Map H4 • 28102 22218 • www.cretanvillas.gr • €€€€€

General Index

Acknowledgments

The Author
Robin Gauldie is a freelance travel writer and photographer based in the UK.

Contributions
Carol Edwards

Produced by BLUE ISLAND PUBLISHING

Editorial Director
Rosalyn Thiro

Art Director
Stephen Bere

Associate Editor
Michael Ellis

Designer
Lee Redmond

Picture Research
Ellen Root

Research Assistance
Amaia Allende

Main Photographers
Robin Gauldie,
Nigel Hicks

Index
Jane Simmonds

Fact Checkers
Michelle Crawford,
Liz and Paul Marsden

AT DORLING KINDERSLEY

Publisher
Douglas Amrine

Publishing Manager
Helen Townsend

Managing Art Editor
Ian Midson

Revisions Team
Emma Anacootee, Emer FitzGerald, Jo Gardner, Prerna Gupta, Victoria Heyworth-Dunne, Jacky Jackson, Sumita Khatwani, Rahul Kumar, Maite Lantaron, Darren Longley, Paul Marsden, Helen Partington, Rada Radojicic, Marisa Renzullo, Sands Publishing Solutions, Liz Sharp, Avantika Sukhia, Ajay Verma, Deepika Verma, Karen Villabona, Dora Whitaker

Senior Cartographic Editor
Casper Morris

Senior DTP Designer
Jason Little

Senior Production Controller
Sarah Dodd

Picture Credits

Additional Photography
Max Alexander, Joe Cornish, Philip Gatward, Derek Hall, David Murray, Rob Reichenfeld, Tony Souter, Clive Streeter.

The publishers would like to thank all the museums, archaeological sites, churches, monasteries, hotels, restaurants, bars, clubs, shops, galleries and other establishments for their assistance and kind permission to photograph.

Placement Key: a - above; b - below/bottom; c - centre; f - far; l - left; r - right; t - top

AKG, LONDON: 32tl, 33tl, 59tl; Eric Lessing 32c, 56c, 58tr, 58c; ALAMY IMAGES: Glen Allison 75clb; Steve Outram 68tl; Elaine Rhodes 70tc; Kevin Wheal 14cl; LH Images 36tr; IML Image Grouup 72br; ALCANEA CAFE & WINE BAR: 100tl; ANCIENT ART AND ARCHITECTURE: 57r; ARDEA: 60tc; Bob Gibbons 52tr; Pascal Goetcheluch 54tr;

ARGYROPOULOS PRESS PHOTO: 60tl, 61r, 62tl, 62b, 63tl; AVLI: 68bl.

BRIDGEMAN ART LIBRARY: Fitzwilliam Museum, University of Cambridge, Pietro da Cortona's *Allegory of the Labours of Hercules* 58tl; Museo Archaeologico, Bari 8b; Musée de Petit Palais, Avignon, France, Peter of the Campana Cassoni's, *Defeat of Athens by Minos, King of Crete* (panel) 56tl; Sto Tome, Toledo, Spain, El Greco's *Self Portrait*, (detail from the *Burial of Count Orgaz*, 1586–8) 56b.

CASA VENETA: 128tl; CORBIS: Yann Arthus-Bertrand 46c; CHRISTIE'S IMAGES: 32b; Gallo Images 54tl.

DREAMSTIME.COM: Arsty 79cr; Fer737ng 24-25c.

MARC DUBIN: 52tl, 52c.

ELEONAS COTTAGES: 130tc.

GETTY IMAGES/HULTON ARCHIVE: Danita Delimont 37cr; Robert Harding World Imagery/Marco Simoni 94tl; Topical Press Agency 57tl.

HISTORICAL AND ART MUSEUM, RETHYMNO: 38b.

COURTESY OF KAZANTZAKIS PUBLICATIONS: 56tr.

COURTESY OF LYCHNOSTASIS OPEN AIR MUSEUM: 38c.

HANS MAAGDELIJN: 71tl; IAIN MCGREGOR: 112bl.

NATALIA'S HOUSES: 128tc; NHPA: Dr. Eckart Pott 54b; Karl Switak 55tl.

STEVE OUTRAM: 38tc, 50tl, 50b, 52b.

RESTAURANT CAFE PARADISO: 88bc. ROBERTHARDING.COM: Nelly Boyd 63r; Ken Gillham 61tl; Loraine Wison 47tl; Trevor Wood 53t.

STOCKPHOTO: 60tr/c/b, 66bl, 67tl; STRATOS VILLAS: 131tl; SYNAGOGI BAR: 100tc.

TO PETRINO: 88bl; TRAVEL LIBRARY: Philip Enticknap 62tr/ca.

PETER WILSON: 46b, 50tr.

All other images are © Dorling Kindersley. For further information see www.dkimages.com.

Cartography Credits
Martin Darlison (Encompass Graphics Ltd)

Crete map derived from East View Cartographic database: www.cartographic.com

Special Editions of DK Travel Guides

DK Travel Guides can be purchased in bulk quantities at discounted prices for use in promotions or as premiums. We are also able to offer special editions and personalized jackets, corporate imprints, and excerpts from all of our books, tailored specifically to meet your own needs.

To find out more, please contact:
(in the United States) **SpecialSales@dk.com**
(in the UK) **TravelSpecialSales@uk.dk.com**
(in Canada) DK Special Sales at **general@tourmaline.ca**
(in Australia) **business.development@pearson.com.au**

Phrase Book

In an Emergency

Help!	**Voítheia!**	vo-ee-theea!
Stop!	**Stamatíste!**	sta-ma-tee-steh!
Call a doctor!	**Fonáxte éna giatró!**	fo-na-ksteh e-na ya-tro!
Call an ambulance/ the police/ fire brigade!	**Kaléste to asthenofóro/ tin astynomía/tin pyrosvestikí!**	ka-le-steh to as-the-no-fo-ro/ teen a-sti-no-the mía/teen pee-ro-zve-stee-kee!
Where is the nearest telephone/ hospital/ pharmacy?	**Poú eínai to plisiéstero tiléfono/ nosokomeío/ farmakeío?**	poo ee-ne to ste-ro tee-le-pho-no/ no-so-ko-mee-o/ far-ma-kee-o?

Communication Essentials

Yes	**Nai**	neh
No	**Ochi**	o-chee
Please	**Parakaló**	pa-ra-ka-lo
Thank you	**Efcharistó**	ef-cha-ree-sto
You are welcome	**Parakaló**	pa-ra-ka-lo
OK/alright	**Entáxei**	en-da-ksee
Excuse me	**Me synchoreíte**	me seen-cho-ree-teh
Hello	**Geiá sas**	yeea sas
Goodbye	**Antío**	an-dee-o
Good morning	**Kaliméra**	ka-lee-me-ra
Good night	**Kalin'ychta**	ka-lee-neech-ta
Morning	**Proí**	pro-ee
Afternoon	**Apógevma**	a-po-yev-ma
Evening	**Vrádi**	vrath-i
This morning	**Símera to proí**	see-me-ra to pro-ee
Yesterday	**Chthés**	chthes
Today	**Símera**	see-me-ra
Tomorrow	**Avrio**	av-ree-o
Here	**Edó**	ed-o
There	**Ekeí**	e-kee
What?	**Tí?**	tee?
Why?	**Giatí?**	ya-tee?
Where?	**Poú?**	poo?
How?	**Pós?**	pos?
Wait!	**Perímene!**	pe-ree-me-neh!
How are you?	**Tí káneis?**	tee ka-nees?
Very well, thank you.	**Poly kalá, efcharistó.**	po-lee ka-la, ef-cha-ree-sto.
How do you do?	**Pós eíste?**	pos ees-te?

Pleased to meet you.	**Chaíro pol'y.**	che-ro po-lee.
What is your name?	**Pós légeste?**	pos le-ye-ste?
Where is/are…?	**Poú eínai…?**	poo ee-neá?
How far is it to…?	**Póso apéchei…?**	po-so a-pe-chee?
How do I get to..?	**Pós mporó na páo…?**	pos bo-ro-na pa-o…?
Do you speak English?	**Miláte Angliká?**	mee-la-te an-glee-ka?
I understand.	**Katalavaíno.**	ka-ta-la-ve-no.
I don't understand	**Den katalavaíno.**	then ka-ta-la-ve-no.
Could you speak slowly?	**Miláte lígo pio argá parakaló?**	mee-la-te lee-go pyo ar-ga pa-ra-ka-lo?
I'm sorry.	**Me synchoreíte.**	me seen-cho-ree teh.
Does anyone have a key?	**Echei kanénas kleidí?**	e-chee ka-ne-nas klee-dee?

Useful Words

big	**Megálo**	me-ga-lo
small	**Mikró**	mi-kro
hot	**Zestó**	zes-to
cold	**Kr'yo**	kree-o
good	**Kaló**	ka-lo
bad	**Kakó**	ka-ko
enough	**Arketá**	ar-ke-ta
well	**Kalá**	ka-la
open	**Anoichtá**	a-neech-ta
closed	**Kleistá**	klee-sta
left	**Aristerá**	a-ree-ste-ra
right	**Dexiá**	dek-see-a
straight on	**Eftheía**	ef-thee-a
between	**Anámesa/ Metax'y**	a-na-me-sa/ me-tak-see
on the corner of..	**Sti gonía tou…**	stee go-nee-a too
near	**Kontá**	kon-da
far	**Makriá**	ma-kree-a
up	**Epáno**	e-pa-no
down	**Káto**	ka-to
early	**Norís**	no-rees
late	**Argá**	ar-ga
entrance	**I eísodos**	ee ee-so-thos
exit	**I éxodos**	ee e-kso-dos
toilet occupied/ engaged	**Oi toualétes / Kateiliméni**	ee-too-a-le-tes ka-tee-lee-me-nee

---

Note: words in bold (centre columns) are transliterated according to the system used by the Greek Government. However, this system is not used consistently throughout Crete, and visitors will encounter many variants on road signs, menus etc.

unoccupied	**Eléftheri**	e-lef-the-ree
free/no charge	**Doreán**	tho-re-**an**
in/out	**Mésa/Exo**	me-sa/**ek**-so

Making a Telephone Call

Where is the nearest public telephone?	**Poú vrísketai o plisiésteros tilefonikós thálamos?**	poo vre**es**-ke-teh o plee-see-**e**-ste-ros tee-le-fo-ni-k**os** tha-la-mos?
I would like to place a long-distance call.	**Tha íthela na káno éna yperastikó tilefónima.**	tha **ee**-the-la na ka-no **e**-na ee-pe-ra-sti-k**o** tee-le-fo-nee-ma.
I would like to reverse the charges.	**Tha íthela na chreóso to tilefónima ston paralípti.**	tha **ee**-the-la na chre-**o**-so to tee-le-fo-nee-ma ston pa-ra-lep-tee.
I will try again later.	**Tha xanatilefoníso argótera.**	tha ksa-na-tee-le-fo-n**ee**-so ar-g**o**-te-ra.
Can I leave a message?	**Mporeíte na tou afísete éna mínyma?**	bo-ree-te na too a-fee-se-teh **e**-na mee-nee-ma?
Could you speak up a little please?	**Miláte dynatótera, parakaló?**	mee-**la**-teh dee-na-**to**-te-ra, pa-ra-ka-l**o**?
Hold on.	**Periménete.**	pe-ri-me-ne-teh.
local call	**Topikó tilefónima**	to-pi-k**o** tee-le-fo-nee-ma
OTE telephone office	**O OTE /To tilefoneío**	o O-T**E** /To tee-le-fo-nee-o
phone box/kiosk	**O tilefonikós thálamos**	o tee-le-fo-ni-k**os** tha-la-mos
phone card	**I tilekárta**	ee tee-le-k**a**r-ta

Shopping

How much does this cost?	**Póso kánei?**	p**o**-so ka-nee?
I would like…	**Tha íthela…**	tha **ee**-the-la…
Do you have…?	**Echete…?**	**e**-che-teh?
I am just looking.	**Aplós koitáo.**	a-pl**os** kee-ta-o.
Do you take credit cards/ travellers' cheques?	**travellers' cheques Décheste pistotikés kártes/ travellers' cheques?**	the-ches-teh pee-sto-tee-k**es** kar-tes/ travellers' cheques?
What time do you open/close?	**Póte anoígete/ kleínete?**	p**o**-teh a-nee-ye-teh/ klee-ne-teh?
Can you ship this overseas?	**Mporeíte na to steílete sto exoterikó?**	bo-ree-teh na to stee-le-teh sto e-xo-te-ree k**o**?

This one.	**Aftó edó.**	af-t**o** e-d**o**.
That one.	**Ekeíno.**	e-kee-no.
expensive	**Akrivó**	a-kree-v**o**
cheap	**Fthinó**	fthee-n**o**
size	**To mégethos**	to m**e**-ge-thos
white	**Lefkó**	lef-k**o**
black	**Mávro**	m**a**v-ro
red	**Kókkino**	k**o**-kee-no
yellow	**Kítrino**	k**ee**-tree-no
green	**Prásino**	pra-see-no
blue	**Mple**	bl**e**h

Types of Shop

antique shop	**Magazí me antíkes**	ma-ga-zee me an-dee-kes
bakery	**O foúrnos**	o fo**o**r-nos
bank	**I trápeza**	ee tra-pe-za
bazaar	**To pazári**	to pa-z**a**-ree
bookshop	**To vivliopoleío**	to vee-vlee-o -po-lee-o
butcher	**To kreopoleío**	to kre-o-po-lee-o
cake shop	**To zacharo- plasteío**	to za-cha-ro-pla- stee-o
cheese shop	**Magazí me allantiká**	ma-ga-zee me a-lan-dee-k**a**
department store	**Polykatástima**	Po-lee-ka-ta- stee-ma
fishmarket	**To ichthyopoleío/ psarádiko**	to eech-thee-o- po-lee-o /psa-rá-dee-ko
greengrocer	**To manáviko**	to ma-n**a**-vee-ko
hairdresser	**To kommotírio**	to ko-mo-tee-ree-o
kiosk	**To períptero**	to pe-ree**p**-te-ro
leather shop	**Magazí me dermátina eíd**	ma-ga-zee me ther-ma-tee-na e**e**-thee
street market	**I laïkí agorá**	ee la-e-ke**e** a-go-r**a**
newsagent	**O efimeridopólis**	O e-fee-me- ree-tho-p**o**-lees
pharmacy	**To farmakeío**	to far-ma-ke-o
post office	**To tachydromeío**	to ta-chee- thro-mee-o
shoe shop	**Katástima y podimáton**	ka-t**a**-stee-ma ee-po-dee- ma-ton
souvenir shop	**Magazí me "souvenir"**	ma-ga-zee meh "souvenir"
supermarket	**"Supermarket" / Yperagorá**	"Supermarket" / ee-per-a-go-r**a**

Bold letters in the pronunciation guides (right columns) indicate the stressed syllable.

tobacconist	**Eídi kapnistoú**	Ee-thee kap-nees	statue	**To ágalma**	to **a**-gal-ma
travel agent	**To taxeidiotikó grafeío**	to tak-see-thy-o-tee-ko gra-fee-o	theatre	**To théatro**	to the-a-tro
			town hall	**To dimarcheío**	to thee-mar-chee-o

Sightseeing

tourist information	**O EOT**	o E-OT	closed on public holidays	**kleistó tis argíes**	klee-sto tees aryee-es
tourist police	**I touristikí astynomía**	ee too-rees-tee-kee a-stee-no-mee-a			

Transport

archaeological	**archaiologikós**	ar-che-o-lo-yee-kos	When does the ... leave?	**Póte févgei to...?**	po-teh fev-yee to...?
art gallery	**I gkalerí**	ee ga-le-ree	Where is the bus stop?	**Poú eínai i stási tou leoforeíou?**	poo ee-neh ee sta-see too le-o-fo-ree-oo...?
beach	**I paralía**	ee pa-ra-lee-a			
Byzantine	**vyzantinós**	vee-zan-dee-nos	Is there a bus to?	**Ypárchei leoforeío gia...?**	ee-par-chee le-o-fo-ree-o yia...?
castle	**To kástro**	to ka-stro			
cathedral	**I mitrópoli**	ee mee-tro-po-lee	ticket office	**Ekdotíria eisitiríon**	Ek-tho-tee-reea ee-see-tee-ree-on
cave	**To spílaio**	to spee-le-o			
church	**I ekklisía**	ee e-klee-see-a	return ticket	**Eisitírio me epistrofí**	ee-see-tee-ree-o meh e-pee-stro-fee
folk art	**laïkí téchni**	la-ee-kee tech-nee			
fountain	**To syntriváni**	to seen-dree-va-nee	single journey	**Apló eisitírio**	a-plo ee-see-tee-reeo
garden	**O kípos**	o kee-pos	bus station	**O stathmós leoforeíon**	o stath-mos leo-fo-ree-on
gorge	**To farángi**	to fa-ran-gee			
grave of....	**O táfos tou...**	o ta-fos too	bus ticket	**Eisitírio leoforeíou**	ee-see-tee-ree-o leo-fo-ree-oo
hill	**O lófos**	o lo-fos			
historical	**istorikós**	ee-sto-ree-kos	trolley bus	**To trólley**	to tro-le-ee
island	**To nisí**	to nee-see	port	**To limán**	to lee-ma-nee
lake	**I límni**	ee leem-nee	train/metro	**To tréno**	to tre-no
library	**I vivliothíki**	ee veev-lee-o-thee-kee	railway station	**sidirodromikós stathmós**	see-thee-ro-thro-mee-kos stath-mos
mansion	**I épavlis**	ee e-pav-lees			
monastery	**moní**	mo-ni	moped	**To motopodílato/ To michanáki**	to mo-to-po-thee-la-to/to mee-cha-na-kee
mountain	**To vounó**	to voo-no			
municipal	**dimotikós**	thee-mo-tee-kos			
museum	**To mouseío**	to moo-see-o	bicycle	**To podílato**	to po-thee-la-to
national	**ethnikós**	eth-nee-kos	taxi	**To taxí**	to tak-see
park	**To párko**	to par-ko	airport	**To aerodrómio**	to a-e-ro-thro-mee-o
river	**To potámi**	to po-ta-mee			
road	**O drómos**	o thro-mos	ferry	**To "ferry-boat"**	to fe-ree-bot
saint	**ágios/ágioi/ agía/agíes**	a-yee-os/a-yee-ee/a-yee-a/a-yee-es	hydrofoil	**To delfíni / To ydroptérygo**	to del-fee-nee / To ee-throp-te-ree-go
spring	**I pigí**	ee pee-yee			
square	**I plateía**	ee pla-tee-a	catamaran	**To katamarán**	to catamaran
stadium	**To stádio**	to sta-thee-o	for hire	**Enoikiázontai**	e-nee-kya-zon-deh

Note: words in bold (centre columns) are transliterated according to the system used by the Greek Government. However, this system is not used consistently throughout Crete, and visitors will encounter many variants on road signs, menus etc.

Staying in a Hotel

Do you have a vacant room?	**Echete domátia?**	e-che-teh tho-ma-tee-a?
I have a reservation.	**Echo kánei krátisi.**	e-cho ka-nee kra-tee-see.
double room with double bed	**Díklino me dipló kreváti**	thee-klee-no meh thee-plo kre-va-tee
twin room	**Díklino me dipló kreváti**	thee-klee-no meh mo-na kre-vat-ya
single room	**Monóklino**	mo-no-klee-no
room with a bath	**Domátio me mpánio**	tho-ma-tee-o meh ban-yo
shower	**To douz**	To dooz
porter	**O portiéris**	o por-tye-rees
key	**To kleidí**	to klee-dee
room with a sea view/balcony	**Domátio me théa sti thálassa/mpalkóni**	tho-ma-tee-o meh the-a stee tha-la-sa/bal-ko-nee
Does the price include breakfast?	**To proïnó symperilamvánetai stin timí?**	to pro-ee-no seem-ba-ree-lam-va-ne-teh steen tee-mee?

Eating Out

Have you got a table?	**Echete trapézi?**	e-che-te tra-pe-zee?
I want to reserve a table.	**Thélo na kratíso éna trapézi.**	the-lo na kra-tee-so e-na tra-pe-zee.
The bill, please.	**Ton logariazmó parakaló:**	ton lo-gar-yas-mo pa-ra-ka-lo
I am a vegetarian.	**Eímai chortofágos.**	ee-meh chor-to-fa-gos.
What is fresh today?	**Tí frésko échete símera?**	tee fres-ko e-che-teh see-me-ra?
waiter/waitress	**K'yrie/Garson"/Kyría**	Kee-ree-eh/Gar-son/Kee-ree-a
menu	**O katálogos**	o ka-ta-lo-gos
cover charge	**To "couvert"**	to koo-ver
wine list	**O katálogos me ta oinopnevmatódi**	o ka-ta-lo-gos meh ta ee-no-pnev-ma-to-thee
glass	**To potíri**	to po-tee-ree
bottle	**To mpoukáli**	to bou-ka-lee
knife	**To machaíri**	to ma-che-ree
fork	**To piroúni**	to pee-roo-nee
spoon	**To koutáli**	to koo-ta-lee

breakfast	**To proïnó**	to pro-ee-no
lunch	**To mesimerianó**	to me-see-mer-ya-no
dinner	**To deípno**	to theep-no
main course	**To kyríos gévma**	to kee-ree-os yev-ma
starter/first course	**Ta orektiká**	ta o-rek-tee-ka
dessert	**To glykó**	to ylee-ko
dish of the day	**To piáto tís i méras**	to pya-to tees ee-me-ras
bar	**To "bar"**	To bar
taverna	**I tavérna**	ee ta-ver-na
café	**To kafeneío**	to ka-fe-nee-o
fish taverna	**I psarotavérna**	ee psa-ro-ta-ver-na
grill house	**I psistariá**	ee psee-sta-rya
wine shop	**To oinopoleío**	to ee-no-po-lee-o
dairy shop	**To galaktopoleío**	to ga-lak-to-po-lee-o
restaurant	**To estiatório**	to e-stee-a-to-ree-o
ouzeri	**To ouzerí**	to oo-ze-ree
meze shop	**To mezedopoleío**	To me-ze-do-po-lee-o
take away kebabs	**To souvlatzídiko**	To soo-vlat-zee-dee-ko
rare	**Eláchista psiméno**	e-lach-ees-ta psee-me-no
medium	**Métria psiméno**	met-ree-a psee-me-no
well done	**Kalopsiméno**	ka-lo-psee-me-no

Basic Food and Drink

coffee	**O Kafés**	o ka-fes
with milk	**me gála**	me ga-la
black coffee without sugar	**skétos chorís záchari**	ske-tos cho-rees za-cha-ree
medium sweet	**métrios**	me-tree-os
very sweet	**glyk'ys**	glee-kees
tea	**tsái**	tsa-ee
hot chocolate	**zestí sokoláta**	ze-stee so-ko-la-ta
wine	**krasí**	kra-see
red	**kókkino**	ko-kee-no
white	**lefkó**	lef-ko
rosé	**rozé**	ro-ze
raki	**To rakí**	to ra-kee
ouzo	**To oúzo**	to oo-zo

Bold letters in the pronunciation guides (right columns) indicate the stressed syllable.

retsina	**I retsína**	ee ret-see-na	100	**ekató**	e-ka-to
water	**To neró**	to ne-ro	200	**diakósia**	thya-kos-ya
octopus	**To chtapódi**	to chta-po-dee	1,000	**chília**	cheel-ya
fish	**To psári**	to psa-ree	2,000	**d'yo chiliádes**	thee-o cheel-ya-thes
cheese	**To tyrí**	to tee-ree			
halloumi	**To chaloúmi**	to cha-loo-mee	1,000,000	**éna ekatommýrio**	e-na e-ka-to-mee-ree-o
feta	**I féta**	ee fe-ta	one minute	**éna leptó**	e-na lep-to
bread	**To psomí**	to pso-mee	one hour	**mía óra**	mee-a o-ra
bean soup	**I fasoláda**	ee fa-so-la-da	half an hour	**misí óra**	mee-see o-ra
houmous	**To houmous**	to choo-moos	quarter of an hour	**éna tétarto**	e-na te tar-to
halva	**O chalvás**	o chal-vas			
meat kebabs	**O g'yros**	u yee-ros	half past one	**mía kai misí**	mee-a keh mee-see
Turkish delight	**To loukoúmi**	to loo-koo-mee	quarter past one	**mía kai tétarto**	mee-a keh te-tar-to
baklava	**O mpaklavás**	o bak-la-vas	ten past one	**mía kai déka**	mee-a keh the-ka
klephtiko	**To kléftiko**	to klef-tee-ko	quarter to two	**d'yo pará tétarto**	thee-o pa-ra te-tar-to
			ten to two	**d'yo pará déka**	thee-o pa-ra the-ka

Numbers

1	**éna**	e-na	a day	**mía méra**	mee-a me-ra
2	**d'yo**	thee-o	a week	**mía evdomáda**	mee-a ev-tho-ma-tha
3	**tría**	tree-a			
4	**téssera**	te-se-ra	a month	**énas mínas**	e-nas mee-nas
5	**pénte**	pen-deh	a year	**énas chrónos**	e-nas chro-nos
6	**éxi**	ek-si	Monday	**Deftéra**	thef-te-ra
7	**eptá**	ep-ta	Tuesday	**Tríti**	tree-tee
8	**ochtó**	och-to	Wednesday	**Tetárti**	te-tar-tee
9	**ennéa**	e-ne-a	Thursday	**Pémpti**	pemp-tee
10	**déka**	the-ka	Friday	**Paraskeví**	pa-ras-ke-vee
11	**énteka**	en-de-ka	Saturday	**Sávvato**	sa-va-to
12	**dódeka**	tho-the-ka	Sunday	**Kyriakí**	keer-ee-a-kee
13	**dekatría**	de-ka-tree-a	January	**Ianouários**	ee-a-noo-a-ree-os
14	**dekatéssera**	the-ka-tes-se-ra	February	**Fevrouários**	fev-roo-a-ree-os
15	**dekapénte**	the-ka-pen-de	March	**Mártios**	mar-tee-os
16	**dekaéxi**	the-ka-ek-si	April	**Aprílios**	a-pree-lee-os
17	**dekaeptá**	the-ka-ep-ta	May	**Máios**	ma-ee-os
18	**dekaochtó**	the-ka-och-to	June	**Ioúnios**	ee-oo-nee-os
19	**dekaennéa**	the-ka-e-ne-a	July	**Ioúlios**	ee-oo-lee-os
20	**eíkosi**	ee-ko-see	August	**Avgoustos**	av-goo-stos
21	**eikosiéna**	ee-ko-see-e-na	September	**Septémvrios**	sep-tem-vree-os
30	**triánta**	tree-an-da	October	**Októvrios**	ok-to-vree-os
40	**saránta**	sa-ran-da	November	**Noémvrios**	no-em-vree-os
50	**penínta**	pe-neen-da	December	**Dekémvrios**	the-kem-vree-os
60	**exínta**	ek-seen-da			
70	**evdomínta**	ev-tho-meen-da			
80	**ogdónta**	og-thon-da			
90	**enenínta**	e-ne-neen-da			

Note: words in bold (centre columns) are transliterated according to the system used by the Greek Government. However, this system is not used consistently throughout Crete, and visitors will encounter many variants on road signs, menus etc.